W9-DED-195

MODERN HEROES

CORRIE TEN BOOM / ERIC LIDDELL
BILLY GRAHAM / LUIS PALAU

BARBOUR
PUBLISHING, INC.
Uhrichsville, Ohio

© 2001 by Barbour Publishing, Inc.

ISBN 1-58660-128-8

Corrie ten Boom by Kjersti Hoff Baez. © 1989 by Barbour Publishing, Inc.
Eric Liddell by Ellen Caughey. © 2000 by Barbour Publishing, Inc.
Billy Graham by Sam Wellman. © 1997 by Sam Wellman.
Luis Palau by W. Terry Whalin. © 1998 by Barbour Publishing, Inc.

All Scripture quotations, unless otherwise noted, are taken from the King James Version of the Bible.

Scripture quotations marked NIV are taken from the HOLY BIBLE, NEW INTERNATIONAL VERSION®. NIV®. Copyright © 1973, 1978, 1984 by International Bible Society. Used by permission of Zondervan Publishing House. All rights reserved.

All Scripture quotations marked RSV are from the Revised Standard Version of the Bible, copyright 1946, 1952, 1971 by the Division of Christian Education of the National Council of the Churches of Christ in the USA. Used by permission.

Scripture quotations marked NKJV are taken from the New King James Version. Copyright © 1979, 1980, 1982 by Thomas Nelson, Inc. Used by permission. All rights reserved.

All rights reserved. No part of this publication may be reproduced or transmitted in any form or by any means without written permission of the publisher.

Published by Barbour Publishing, Inc., P.O. Box 719, Uhrichsville, OH 44683
http://www.barbourbooks.com

Member of the
Evangelical Christian
Publishers Association

Printed in the United States of America.

CONTENTS

CORRIE TEN BOOM

HEROINE OF HAARLEM

by Kjersti Hoff Baez

CHAPTER 1

Casper ten Boom stood looking into the cradle with love brimming over in his heart. It was April 15, 1892, and another little ten Boom had been born into the world. Born prematurely, the baby was tiny, and her skin was a bluish color. They named her Cornelia.

The room was filled with aunts and uncles who hovered over the cradle, clucking like hens.

"She'll never make it through the night."

"She's just too weak."

Casper scooped the baby into his arms and shook his head. "She will be just fine," he said. "And we shall call her Corrie."

Cor smiled at her husband and leaned back on her pillows. She whispered a prayer of thanks to God for her newest child. The baby whimpered, and at the sound of her weak little cry, Casper handed Corrie back to her mother. Cor wrapped another blanket around the baby and lulled her to sleep.

Between the warmth of the blankets and the love of the ten Boom family, little Corrie grew stronger every day. Betsie, Willem, and Nollie were delighted to have a new sister, and the months flew by.

Like his father before him, Casper ten Boom was a watchmaker. Casper worked in the Dutch city of Amsterdam, but when his father died, they moved to the city of Haarlem so he could take over his father's business. The shop was located on a street called the Barteljorisstraat in an old building called the Beje.

The Beje was a unique house. It was, in fact, a combination of two buildings. The larger building faced the Barteljorisstraat and housed the watch shop and workroom on the first floor. The second and third floors comprised the parlor and five tiny bedrooms. The smaller building in the back of this was also three stories high, but its floor levels did not match with the floor levels of the front building. A twisting stairway connected the buildings, making the house seem more like a complicated puzzle than a home.

Life at the Beje settled into a happy routine, with Casper busy in the shop and the rooms upstairs always brimming with people. Cor's three sisters lived at the Beje with the ten Booms. Every morning after breakfast and every evening after dinner, Casper would bring out the old family Bible and read a passage to his family. The Scriptures were as vital to the ten Boom household as food, and their love for Christ spilled over into the lives of all who crossed the threshold of the Beje.

Casper ten Boom worked very hard in his watch shop and eventually became known as the best watchmaker in Holland. His reputation even reached beyond Holland, and it was not uncommon to see young men from other countries come to the Beje to apply for a job as an apprentice.

But it was not his excellent skills as a watchmaker that endeared Mr. ten Boom to the people of Haarlem. His kind and loving spirit was the key to his popularity; the genuine presence of Christ shone in him. No matter what a person's outward position in society—great or small, young or old—Casper ten Boom loved and accepted everyone.

Casper and Cor prayed earnestly that all their children would serve the Lord. In the midst of cooking and cleaning, Cor ten Boom used every opportunity to bring her children to Christ. When five-year-old Corrie was playing house and visiting the home of an imaginary friend, Corrie's mother told her about a real friend named Jesus Who would enter the home of her heart if Corrie would only invite Him in. The little girl with the big blue eyes nodded yes and on the wings of prayer through simple faith, Corrie was born into the kingdom of God.

Corrie and Nollie were close in age, so they often played together in the Beje. One day they paused in their play as the sound of their mother's voice reached their ears.

"Corrie, Nollie!" she called to them from the kitchen. "Are you coming with me to Mrs. Hoog's?"

Mrs. Hoog's baby had died, and Mrs. ten Boom was quick to respond to another's grief. She grabbed her coat and the package of food she had prepared and started for the door. A flurry of footsteps sounded behind her as the two girls followed her out of the house.

Nollie and Corrie volunteered to accompany their mother

more out of curiosity than concern. The two girls had never seen anyone dead before, and it was customary to keep the deceased in the home for viewing before the burial.

The girls walked behind their mother, whispering nervously to each other.

"Are you scared?" Corrie asked Nollie.

"Of course not," Nollie responded, knees knocking.

"Me neither," said Corrie, her little hands trembling.

Once inside Mrs. Hoog's, Mrs. ten Boom gathered the young mother in her arms and comforted her without saying a word. Corrie and Nollie stared at the crib with the dead baby in it. Nollie convinced Corrie to touch it, and Corrie was not prepared for the terrible coldness of the baby's skin.

After what seemed like centuries, Momma finally said good-bye to Mrs. Hoog and led her girls out the door. Corrie and Nollie held their mother's hands and practically dragged her home to the Beje.

Corrie ran up the familiar winding stairway to her bedroom and threw herself upon the bed, weeping.

The sound of her weeping brought her father to her side. Corrie explained between sobs the terror of death and how frightened she was that everyone was going to die.

Casper spoke reassuringly to his little girl. He told her God was well able to handle our fears if we would trust Him. Even the deepest fear could not separate us from God. In His own way, in His own time, He would take care of all our needs.

"Nothing can separate us from His love, Corrie. This is

His promise to us. Not even death can separate us from Him." Casper pulled out his handkerchief and wiped his daughter's tears away.

Corrie looked up into her father's face and gazed at his sparkling blue eyes. She felt completely safe with him nearby. She closed her eyes and listened to the ticking of the many watches that Casper always carried in his vest pockets. For a moment, the little girl sensed that there was something more in her little room than just her earthly father. For a moment, Corrie sensed the unmeasurable love of her heavenly Father surrounding her.

Discovering how wide and high and deep that love truly is would be the adventure of a lifetime.

CHAPTER 2

Corrie was six, and it was time for her to begin school. The thought of going to a strange, new place terrified her, and her young mind searched for ways to avoid the dreadful journey. There must be some way to convince her father and mother that she didn't need to go to school.

Corrie's thoughts were interrupted by the chiming of the clocks in the shop below. The sounds echoed in the halls of the Beje, announcing that it was time for the ten Boom children to go to school. Willem, Betsie, and Nollie bustled out the door, but Corrie didn't move. All the adults in the house tried to explain to the little girl the importance of an education and how she must go to school at once, but it was Casper who eased the child out of the house and down the Barteljorisstraat to the elementary school. Corrie was still scared, but with her father by her side, she knew that somehow she would survive the ordeal.

Corrie did survive her first day and her first year of school. In the years that followed, she enjoyed her studies, but at times couldn't resist a daydream of a scheme to play a trick on the teacher. Her path crossed with the principal's more than once, and she and her cousin Dot enjoyed many childhood adventures together.

Education continued at home, too. Casper devised games

to teach his children other languages. As a result, Corrie learned French, German, and English. Casper and Cor taught their children to love music, and many evenings were spent singing together at the old piano.

Education was very important in the ten Boom household, but it was also important to share what one learned with others. Once of Corrie's aunts, Tante Jans, taught the girls to sing hymns to Dutch soldiers who lived in Haarlem. Betsie, Corrie's oldest sister, was a marvelous storyteller, and she taught Corrie how to teach the Bible to children.

One morning, seventeen-year-old Corrie awoke feeling dizzy. She tried to focus her eyes on the walls of the tiny room she shared with Nollie, but the walls wouldn't stay still and Corrie fell back on her pillow.

"Corrie, are you all right?" Nollie stared at Corrie's ashen face.

Corrie tried to sit up again, but the fever wouldn't let her. The room swirled around her in a dizzying dance. Nollie ran to get Momma. The doctor was summoned, and after he left, Casper climbed the stairs to Corrie's room to tell her the doctor's diagnosis. It wasn't going to be easy.

"Well, Poppa, what did he say?" Corrie asked as her father entered the bedroom. She was feeling awfully weak, but surely this was just a case of the flu. Her heart began to pound, however, as Casper looked sadly into his daughter's eyes.

"He says you have tuberculosis." Corrie closed her eyes in terror. She knew the disease was deadly.

Corrie was confined to her bed for several months, and her family prayed faithfully for her every day. It was a struggle for Corrie to accept what had happened; she longed to be out serving the Lord, singing and teaching. But she knew it was useless to argue with God, so she prayed, "Thy will be done, not mine."

The months passed slowly and one day the doctor came to reexamine Corrie. His face lit up with relief as he triumphantly related the news to Corrie and her family.

"Appendicitis, my dear! You don't have tuberculosis; you have appendicitis! I shall operate right away, and you will be as good as new!" Corrie wept for joy and her room filled up with family as everyone gathered around her bed to rejoice over the good news. Corrie knew God's hand was on her life, and He was well able to help her through any trial.

The years that followed brought many changes to the Beje. Willem graduated from the University of Leiden and became a minister. He married a girl named Tine van Veen. Nollie chose to be a schoolteacher. Betsie worked in the shop for Casper, taking care of the books and the customers. Corrie helped Tante Anna run the busy household of the Beje.

From 1914 to 1918, World War I rocked Europe, but Holland remained neutral throughout the ordeal. To fight against the fears of those uncertain days, the ten Booms used the best tool they had: prayer. They prayed for all those who were fighting and prayed for the war to end. When the war did end, they put their prayers into action by taking foster children into the Beje. Many people all over Europe were starving for food and compassion. Germany was especially needy, and the ten Booms' foster children were all from Germany.

Not long after the war, Momma ten Boom suffered a stroke that made her an invalid. No longer able to speak aloud, she spoke her love through her eyes. Corrie was amazed at the peace that radiated from her mother's face. A paralyzed body could not stop the love inside Mrs. ten Boom from reaching others through that all-important tool—prayer.

Corrie remembered her bout with appendicitis and what a struggle it had been for her to accept being stuck in bed for months. Now, before her eyes, her mother was unable to move or speak, and yet she was still a shining vessel of God's love.

"Dear Momma," Corrie said gently, looking into her mother's sparkling eyes. "How do you do it? How can you be so happy?"

Momma smiled up at her, and her eyes seemed to say, *"All is well, for I am in the hands of my Lord. He will use me as I am, and in Him I rejoice."*

The line from a poem by John Milton traced the air with its truth: "They also serve, who only stand and wait."

Willem and Tine lived in the town of Hilversum, and Corrie liked to visit them, especially as their home began to be filled with children. On one visit to see Willem, Corrie met one of Willem's friends from the university. His name was Karel, and as Corrie was being introduced, her heart began to pound and her hands started to tremble. She hid her hands behind her back and mumbled a hello.

"Are you all right?" Willem asked his sister. Her face was flushed with color.

Corrie was in love.

From that day on, Corrie and Karel spent as much time together as they could. They talked about everything, and it seemed to Corrie that they were perfect for each other. She was incredibly happy. When she thought of starting her own family with Karel, she could hardly contain herself. Willem, however, did not seem so happy about the new relationship.

Finally, Willem broke the news to Corrie. "He will never marry you, Corrie," Willem said softly. "He can't."

"What are you talking about?" Corrie cried out. Fear swept her heart, and she became short of breath.

Willem explained that Karel's parents wanted him to marry someone wealthy, someone with a high position in society. The ten Boom family was definitely poor, and though well loved by the city of Haarlem, they were not high-society people.

Corrie hoped Willem was wrong, but several months later an announcement arrived from the church Karel was pastoring. It was an engagement announcement.

The pain in Corrie's heart was unbearable. All she could picture in her mind was this rich young lady marrying Karel, her Karel. But even as she poured out her grief in sobs, Corrie knew Karel was not hers. He belonged to the Lord, and Corrie belonged to the Lord, too. His plans for her would never fail, and He knew what was best for Corrie ten Boom.

Corrie busied herself at the Beje and tried not to think of Karel. She prayed often, and as she surrendered her life to the Lord, Corrie's heart filled with peace. She knew whatever the Lord had planned for her would be good and fulfilling.

The day arrived when Nollie was married to a schoolteacher named Flip. She moved out of the Beje into a house on Bos en Hoven Street. Corrie was glad Nollie lived nearby. It was hard to see her go. The Beje was getting to be too quiet. All three aunts had passed away, and the day came when Momma left the Beje, too. Corrie looked around at the empty rooms and was tempted to fall into despair.

Casper laid a reassuring hand on his youngest daughter's shoulder.

"We shall see Momma again. You know that I miss her, too, but Corrie dear, the best is yet to be."

When Betsie became ill, Corrie took over her work in the watch shop. She loved her new job, and the two ten Boom sisters decided to trade jobs. Betsie took over the house and soon had it running smoothly. Following in her mother's footsteps, Betsie was always busy cooking something for someone in need. She decorated the house with color and flowers; she loved her new occupation.

Meanwhile, in the shop, Corrie was making a discovery about herself. She loved the business world. She enjoyed going over the books and dealing with the customers. As she watched her father bent over his workbench, repairing a watch with great precision and skill, a desire began to grow within her.

"Father, I want to be a watchmaker."

Casper looked up at her from his bench. In those days it was customary for the son to take up the family trade, but that did not stop Casper and Corrie.

"We will begin your training tomorrow."

Casper trained Corrie at the shop and then sent her to Switzerland to work in a watch factory. There Corrie learned more about putting watches together. French was the only language spoken there, and Corrie was glad her father had insisted his children learn other languages. She returned to Haarlem and received her license to make watches. Corrie was the first woman in Holland to be a licensed watchmaker.

There was more to life than the watch shop, however. Casper was constantly sharing his faith with everyone he met. He preached the gospel whenever the door was opened to do so and held Bible studies for anyone who was interested. There were always people in the watch shop with Casper, telling him their problems and waiting for his wise counsel. Corrie watched and listened as her father treated each person with the utmost respect, whether the person was a statesmen or a servant.

With Betsie's help, Corrie started a club for young teenaged girls. Corrie's faith in God was infectious, and many girls came to Christ through the clubs. There were all kinds of activities and projects, and news of the fun the girls were having spread throughout Haarlem.

Eventually, Corrie started a "Friends" club that included both girls and boys and was a great success. Over the years boys and girls alike enjoyed the fun of the clubs and listened as Corrie and other leaders taught them about the Lord. For many of them, the influence of the clubs would change their lives. They learned that God was near to anyone who called on His name, and this wonderful God had a plan for their lives.

Corrie loved working with the teenagers, but there was a Bible school she led that was very dear to her heart, a Bible class for mentally retarded children. The children received the Lord and His Word with sincere hearts. Their intense love and faith in Christ were an encouragement to Corrie's own love and faith.

Betsie, Corrie, and their father spent the years enjoying the Lord and serving Him. Willem and Tine had four children, and Flip and Nollie had six; the grandchildren added great happiness to their days. Corrie was grateful for the life God had given the ten Booms.

The watch shop had two other permanent workers besides Casper and Corrie. A lady named Toos was the clerk for the shop, and an old man named Christoffels worked for Casper as a clock mender.

In 1937, the city of Haarlem joined in the hundredth anniversary of the ten Boom watch shop. It was in 1837 that Casper ten Boom's father had first opened up shop on the street called Barteljorisstraat. The Beje was bursting at the seams with people from all walks of life who came to celebrate and filled the Beje with affection for Haarlem's "Grand Old Man."

The joy of the occasion was dampened, however, when Willem arrived with a young Jewish man from Germany. The man's face was horribly burned. Willem explained that the man had been terrorized by a group of German teenagers.

"I'm afraid this is just the beginning," Willem said, pointing to the man's face. "This is part of the evil that has swallowed Germany whole."

The guests shuddered, but the party continued. It appeared that many in Holland—indeed in the rest of the free world—had chosen to ignore the alarming symptoms that were surfacing in Germany. There was a powerful man in Germany that very few believed would be of any importance in world history. His name was Adolf Hitler.

The shadows of evening embraced the day and lulled it to sleep. The guests left and the Beje was quiet. Corrie sighed with satisfaction. It had been a wonderful party. But the memory of Willem's guest popped up in her mind and wouldn't leave her alone.

After the celebration, the routine at the Beje returned to normal. After the daily Scripture reading at 8:30, Christoffels, Toos, and Corrie followed the old watchmaker down the twisting stairs to the workshop. Betsie remained upstairs and cleared the breakfast dishes.

Once inside the shop, Corrie and Toos opened the shutters to let in the morning light. Casper and Christoffels settled down on their workbenches in the workroom. The early rays of the sun rested on the display case and reflected off the gold and silver watches that lay there. Corrie loved this time of day. The sun's light was always brand-new. *New every morning,* she thought to herself. *What a perfect picture of God's love—new every morning.*

"Isn't it a gorgeous day, Toos?" Corrie spoke to her fellow worker with great enthusiasm.

Toos only grunted and began to dust the display case.

Oh well, thought Corrie. *It's a beautiful day anyway!* She went back into the workroom to the desk where she handled the bookkeeping for the shop. This never failed to be a source of frustration for her. It wasn't the books that frustrated her; it was the way her father conducted business. Casper ten Boom was definitely not a businessman. A master craftsman, yes; a businessman, no.

Corrie opened the black ledger on her desk and carefully checked the list of sales. Shaking her head in exasperation, she turned to speak to her father. He was bent over his workbench, intently examining the insides of a gold pocket watch from Germany.

"Marvelous! A work of art, that's what it is," he whispered aloud, gently cleaning the tiny wheels and screws of the golden watch.

"Father," Corrie called to him.

"Yes, my dear." Casper stopped what he was doing and looked at his daughter. "What is it?"

"Did you finish the job on the van der Veen watch?"

"Let me see," he mused, tugging on his beard. "You mean the Swiss watch with the engraving on the back? A splendid little machine!"

"Did you finish working on it?" Corrie tried hard not to let her voice betray her impatience.

"Oh, yes. Mrs. van der Veen picked it up last Thursday. A lovely lady, Mrs. van der Veen. Did you know her son is studying to be a doctor?"

"Father!" Corrie interrupted what was sure to be a twenty-minute discussion of the van der Veen family. "Did she pay you? What did you charge her?"

Casper smiled at Corrie, his eyes as true blue as when he was born seventy-nine years before. "Corrie, how could I charge her? That watch is an antique, you know, and has been in the van der Veen family for many, many years." He cleared his throat with enthusiasm. "It first belonged to Hans van der Veen and he—"

"Oh Father!" Corrie cut him off with a groan. "Did you at least give her a bill?"

Casper laughed and returned to his work. "What a worry-wart you are, my dear!"

Corrie sighed and turned back to her books. *It's a wonder we haven't gone bankrupt,* she thought. *Sometimes I think he's too generous.*

And yet she knew they always managed to do more than just make ends meet. Yes, there were some who took advantage of Casper's generosity, but many of their customers did pay their bills, and things had a way of working out. From Momma's stove to Poppa's workbench, the ten Booms were known as a giving family. Momma's love and soups had comforted many a weary soul, and the watchmaker's wise counsel had helped repair many a broken heart. This was not because the ten Booms were givers by nature, but because the greatest giver of all lived in their hearts and home.

The doorbell in the alley jangled impatiently, and Corrie hurried to the hall behind the workshop to open the door. A delivery boy handed Corrie a pile of packages and tipped his hat. She reached into her dress pocket for the tip, but to her surprise, a hand reached out from behind her and paid the boy.

Corrie swung around and was immediately surrounded by two strong arms.

"Willem!" She laughed and kissed his bearded face. "What are you doing here?"

Placing his hands on her shoulders, he gently directed her toward the shop. "Back to work, little sister."

Corrie laughed. "Little sister, indeed! At forty-five years of age, I'm not exactly a schoolgirl!"

Corrie's laughter reached the workshop before she did, and Casper looked up from his workbench.

"I see you've run into your brother, Corrie!" Casper's eyes twinkled behind his wire-rimmed glasses as he surveyed his two children. Corrie placed the pile of packages on her desk.

"Yes, Father. He's teasing me as usual, and. . ." She stopped in midsentence. All of the packages were stamped with a message in bold red letters: "Return to Sender."

"Why, these are all the packages we sent to Germany this month. I don't understand it. We've done business with these suppliers for years! I wonder what in the world. . ." Her voice trailed off and she sighed. Another frustration to be faced. German watches were among the finest watches in Europe, and the ten Boom shop sold many of them in the course of a year.

"Let me see the packages, Corrie." Willem's tone was strangely serious. He picked up the packages, glancing at the address on each one.

"What do you notice about the names on these boxes, Corrie?" he asked sternly.

Suddenly, Corrie felt like a little schoolgirl again, being questioned by her older brother. She looked at the addresses, but nothing clicked. Willem's tone of voice disturbed her, and she was unable to think straight.

"I don't know, Will, I can't tell. . ."

"Read the names! The names!" Willem's anger exploded in the air, and Corrie stared at him, shocked. All eyes were on Willem. Even Toos ran in from the shop to see what was the matter. Casper ten Boom's voice penetrated the bizarre scenario.

"What is the meaning of this, my son? What are you trying to say?"

The sound of his father's voice settled onto Willem's anger like snow on a fire, and as quickly as the anger had come, it flickered out. Willem reached over and took Corrie by the hand.

"I'm sorry, my dear Corrie. It's just that. . ." He stopped and pointed to the names on the packages. "Look—Kaufman,

Rubenstein, Lieberman—don't you see?"

"Why, those are all Jewish names, Willem." Casper looked at his son with wondering eyes.

"Yes, Father. All Jewish."

"But I still don't understand," Corrie stammered.

"The Nazi movement in Germany is no longer just a terrible idea. The German leaders are putting into practice what Adolf Hitler has hammered into their heads. The Jews are considered to be subhuman enemies of the German nation. All over Germany, Jews are disappearing."

Corrie and Casper looked at each other, not wanting to believe what they were hearing. But deep inside, they knew Willem was right. Ten years before, while studying for his doctorate in Germany, Willem had written a paper warning people of a dark way of thinking that was quietly invading the German universities. No one believed him then, but now it was all too real.

Willem cleared his throat and made a feeble attempt to sound cheerful.

"Our nursing home in Hilversum is overflowing now with Jewish refugees. With God's help, we will be able to take care of them until this madness ends."

"If we can be of any help, my son, let us know." Casper sat down at his workbench and resumed his study of the German watch. The laughter that had filled the air only moments before was gone now. In its place there hung a heavy sadness.

Corrie slipped her hand around Willem's arm. "Won't

you stay and have lunch with us?"

"No. Thank you, but I really must be getting back to Hilversum. Tine's got her hands full as it is." He kissed Corrie on the cheek, bade his father good-bye, and was gone.

With a sigh, Corrie returned to her desk and gathered up the packages. Now the bright red lettering glared up at her, symbols of evil. She hastily unwrapped each one and threw the papers in the wastebasket.

The next two years were fairly normal at the Beje. Elsewhere on the European continent, however, things were far from normal. Under the leadership of Adolf Hitler, Germany seized Austria and Czechoslovakia and then set its hungry eyes on the country of Poland. This was sure to spark the outbreak of World War II, and Holland hoped it would maintain the neutral status it had held in World War I. Surely the ugly tentacles of war would not reach over and cross the borders of fair Holland!

In the front room of the ten Boom watch shop, the bell on the door rang loudly as a young man strode into the shop.

"I wish to speak with Mr. Casper ten Boom." He spoke abruptly, looking at Toos impatiently. "Go get him," he commanded.

"And who are you?" Toos asked, ice in her voice. She was not easily flustered, and she took commands from no one except her employer.

The man turned his back on Toos and headed for the workroom. "I'll find him myself."

"You can't go back there!" Toos shouted after him. "Who do you think you are?" She quickly followed after him, her face red with anger. The young man burst into the workroom. At the sight of Mr. ten Boom, he stopped and bowed graciously.

"Mr. ten Boom. My name is Otto Altschuler. I am from Berlin and wish to be your apprentice."

Toos stood behind him, glaring.

"He just barged right in, Casper, and didn't even wait for me to get you. Of all the rude, inconsiderate. . ."

"Now, dear Toos, thank you for showing Mr. Altschuler in. I think I hear the front bell ringing again."

At Casper's gentle prompting, Toos turned on her heel with a huff and stomped back into the watch shop.

"Allow me to introduce my associates," Casper continued. "This is my daughter Corrie. She was the first woman in Holland to become a licensed watchmaker." He beamed with pride. "And this is Christoffels, my highly skilled clock mender." Otto barely nodded at Corrie, and he totally ignored Christoffels.

Casper scanned the papers and nodded in agreement.

"These are excellent recommendations. You can begin work tomorrow. You are welcome to join us at 8:30 for coffee and Bible reading." He shook the young German's hand.

"Thank you, Sir." Otto bowed respectfully and then left as quickly as he had come.

Much to Corrie's relief, the rest of the day ran smoothly.

The January sun retired early, its golden light lingering for a moment over the Barteljorisstraat. The watch shop was empty as Corrie gazed out the front window to savor the last of the day's sunlight. When the sun's rays retreated altogether, she closed the shutters.

Otto was a fast learner, and Casper was delighted with the young man's progress. There was, however, a threatening thread that wove its way through the shop whenever Otto was there. He refused to join the ten Booms for the Bible reading, and although respectful of Mr. ten Boom, Otto treated Christoffels shamefully. Whenever he had the chance (whenever Casper was not in the room), Otto would taunt Christoffels and call him a "worthless old man."

Weeks later, the secretive evil reared its head in full view of the ten Boom family. On a cold winter morning in 1939, just as Casper opened his Bible, shouts rang out in the alleyway. Corrie and Betsie rushed to the alley door and found Christoffels, his face covered with blood.

Mr. Weil, the furrier who lived across the street, handed Corrie the old man's hat. Betsie helped Christoffels up the stairs into the Beje.

"Christoffels! What happened?" Casper hurried over to his colleague.

"It was that apprentice of yours, Casper," Mr. Weil explained. "He pushed the old man into the wall and held him there with all his strength." The furrier's voice boiled over with anger. "It's an outrage! It's not the first time I've seen such goings on! You'd better do something about it, my friend."

Stunned, Casper turned to Christoffels. "Why didn't you tell me this was happening?"

Christoffels said nothing. He was too proud to ask for help from those who loved him best. Casper's heart broke as he thought of the old man being terrorized for weeks by the young German.

"Can you forgive me for being so blind? I had no idea. . . ." Casper's voice trailed off into a tense silence. He left the old man to Betsie's tender care and descended the stairs to the workshop. Corrie followed after him, sensing anger in the air.

They found Otto at his workbench, already busily repairing a Swiss wristwatch. He greeted his employer and resumed his work. Casper put a hand on the young man's shoulder.

"I'm sorry, but you must leave us. There is an old man in my home with blood on his face and terror in his eyes because of you. Surely you must know that the dark road you are traveling leads only to a greater darkness. Turn around, my son, before it is too late."

Corrie trembled in anticipation of an explosion, but Otto was silent. He slammed the door as he left, and father and daughter stood alone in the shop, numb with shock. This was their first face-to-face encounter with the black heart of the Nazi movement.

Corrie hoped it would be their last.

In the spring of 1940, the shadow Adolf Hitler cast over the face of Europe grew deeper and spread itself north to Scandinavia. In April, the German army began its invasion of Norway, seizing the country of Denmark. The little country of Holland still clung to the hope that its neutrality would be honored. On the evening of May 9, people all over Holland gathered around their radios to hear what their prime minister had to say about the fate of their country. Fear of war curled its cold fingers around the hearts of the people.

In the parlor of the Beje, Casper ten Boom and his two daughters waited for the prime minister to speak. Corrie gazed at the radio, remembering evenings long ago when the ten Boom family and friends would gather in the parlor to listen to breathtaking Bach or Beethoven. But Corrie knew tonight there would be no music.

When at last the prime minister's voice crossed the airways, his message was one of peace. Holland would not be invaded but would remain neutral. Betsie and Corrie looked at each other and sighed with relief, but Casper scoffed at the prime minister's words.

"Holland will be invaded," he said. "There is no use denying it."

Casper's words echoed over and over in Corrie's mind as she tossed and turned in her bed that night.

Several hours later, in the cold darkness of the predawn air, German soldiers swiftly and silently parachuted onto Dutch soil near Rotterdam and The Hague. With the help of Dutch Nazi sympathizers, they captured strategic bridges and attacked the nation's airports. At dawn, the Germans launched a ground attack on southern Holland, successfully gaining control of the railroad bridges that spanned the Maas River. Their invasion was complete; they had Holland pinned to the wall.

The sound of an explosion ripped through the air and jolted the city of Haarlem out of its sleep. Betsie and Corrie prayed together, simultaneously, urging the ears of heaven to hear their cry and help save the country. Corrie finally fell silent. She could only weep quietly for her country and her people.

Suddenly before her eyes there passed a vision as clear as a picture on the wall. Corrie saw a wagon drawn by four black horses in the town square. The wagon was filled with people she knew. She saw Father, Willem, her nephew Peter, Toos, and other friends of the family, all seated in the wagon. Betsie was there, and Corrie sat there, also. The horses were taking them somewhere strange and terrifying, but they were helpless to do anything about it.

The vision faded. With a trembling voice, she related the story to Betsie.

Four days later, on May 14, the Germans gave the Dutch an ultimatum: If they did not surrender within twenty-four hours, the Germans would bomb Rotterdam and Utrecht. The Dutch continued to fight, and two hours before the ultimatum was up, the German air force totally destroyed the business section of Rotterdam. The number of civilians whose lives were devastated by the bombing was horrifying:

There were thousands of casualties. Unable to resist the ruthless invader any longer, Holland surrendered.

News of the surrender sent shock waves throughout all of Holland. The unthinkable had become reality. Germany had conquered, and Germany would rule. Immediately, the effects of the new government were felt by the Dutch. No one was allowed on the streets at night after 10 P.M. In order to make purchases in any store, a person had to use ration cards instead of money. Everyone was forced to wear identification cards.

The city of Haarlem watched silently as the Germans marched down its streets to take control. Corrie pulled back the curtain in the shop window and looked up and down the Barteljorisstraat. The street was swarming with soldiers.

"It's like a dream," Corrie whispered. "I can hardly believe what I am seeing."

"It is a nightmare," Toos replied quietly from behind the display case. "It is as if evil is taking over the earth."

Corrie looked at Toos with surprise. The stern old clerk rarely shared her feelings with anyone. Corrie crossed the room and took the old lady by the hand.

"God will see us through this, Toos. No matter what happens, He will be with us."

Toos nodded wordlessly, tears streaming down her face. She retrieved a handkerchief from her pocket, wiped her face, and cleared her throat. "And now, Miss ten Boom," she said formally, "as Casper would say, 'Time for work!' "

Corrie walked back to the workshop to find Nollie's

teenaged son Peter perched on his grandfather's workbench. His face was flushed with anger, and he was speaking loudly to Casper.

"So now what, Grandfather? They are demanding that everyone bring their radios to the department store. What are we going to do about that?"

"Peter, I'm not deaf, yet. Slow down and tell me again—in a normal voice this time." He smiled at his earnest grandson, and Peter made an effort to calm himself.

"What are you talking about, Peter?" Corrie asked. "What's that you said about the radios?"

"The Germans want every Dutchman to bring his radio to the department store downtown. No one will be allowed to have a radio in their home. And I also heard that all telephones will be disconnected. How do you like that?

"They're trying to cut our throats," Peter continued. "We'll be helpless without any way to communicate freely. And I suppose everyone will follow orders, just like a bunch of sheep." He was speaking loudly again, unable to control his anger. Casper put his arm around his troubled grandson.

"First of all, Peter, you must understand that the Germans are in control now. There is not much we can do about that. Your anger is justified, but you must not let it control you. You've got a good head on your shoulders, Peter. Don't let it be ruled by how you feel. If we are to help our country, we must be able to think clearly."

"Yes, Grandfather." Peter got up from the bench and

headed for the stairs. "Guess I'll get something to eat," he mumbled. Corrie's heart went out to him as she listened to him climb the stairs, dragging his feet. Midway up the stairs, the sound of Peter's labored steps ceased on the stairwell.

Corrie started for the door to see what was the matter and was almost knocked over by her nephew as he raced back into the workshop.

"I've got it! I've got it!" he shouted excitedly at Casper. "It's perfect!"

"What on earth are you talking about, Peter? And please, my ears!"

Peter took a deep breath. "I know what to do about the radio! You've got two, don't you?"

"Well, yes. There's the large one in the parlor and the small one Pickwick gave us in the kitchen."

"Right. So, we only turn in one of them!"

"And what, pray tell, do we do with the one we keep?" Corrie asked, shaking her head. "We can't just keep a radio in the house. The Germans are known for their unexpected visits. The radio would have to be invisible!"

"Precisely!" Peter smiled broadly. "Invisible."

"I give up. What are you up to now?" Corrie sat down at her desk and waited for her nephew to explain.

"We will hide the big radio in one of the steps of the stairwell. Those winding old steps are perfect. They'll never find it."

Corrie looked at her father, expecting to see him disapprove of such a plan. Instead, she saw him smile and slap Peter on the back.

"Now that's using your head!" He laughed, picking up the watch he had been working on. "Time for work."

Peter walked back to the stairs and echoed his grandfather's words. "Time for work."

In less than an hour, the secret step was finished. Peter placed the big radio in its new home and grinned in triumph. Corrie and Betsie marveled at Peter's job. Neither of them could tell which step had been tampered with.

"What do you think?" Peter asked his aunts.

"It's fantastic, Peter! You're really quite a wonder!" Betsie gave him a gentle hug.

"Invisible," Corrie replied. "Absolutely invisible!"

"Thank you, thank you." Peter bowed dramatically. "And now, Tante Corrie, it's up to you to carry out the rest of the plan. You must go downtown and turn in the other radio. Remember, it is the only one the ten Booms own." He held her gaze with his serious eyes, and she understood what he was saying to her. Those in charge of collecting the radios would surely ask if this was the only one in the house. Corrie would have to lie.

Several hours later, her mission accomplished, Corrie made her way back to the Beje. Questions flooded her mind. *When a nation is captured and treated cruelly by another nation, what is right and what is wrong?* Corrie wondered what her dear mother would say if she were alive now. Secret steps, hidden radios, and deception—these things were all foreign to Corrie, and yet they seemed necessary in this time of great darkness.

Betsie greeted Corrie at the door in the alley and ushered her into the dining room. She handed her younger sister a cup of hot tea. Seeing the troubled look on Corrie's face, Betsie sought to comfort her.

"We can only do our best, Corrie. The Lord expects nothing more than that. We can only pray that we will have His wisdom in these hard days. He will guide our steps."

Corrie smiled wearily and sipped the hot tea. She watched as Betsie busied herself with the pots on the stove. *I wish I had your strength,* Corrie thought.

CHAPTER 4

The days hurried into months, and the Germans tightened their grip on the Dutch people. The curfew was constantly being changed to an earlier hour until it was almost impossible to go out in the evening. With the approach of winter, food supplies diminished. Meat was rarely available; coffee and tea were unheard-of luxuries. Holland was gray with hunger of body and soul. They looked on with anger and sorrow as many fellow Dutchmen turned their backs on their heritage and joined the National Socialist Bond, the Nazi organization of Holland. Holding out the promise of more food and clothing, the NSB grew in number. The Nazis brought with them their hatred for the Jews, and soon its poison took effect on the streets of Haarlem.

Corrie closed the door in the alley and joined her father on the Barteljorisstraat. Slipping her arm through his, they walked slowly down the narrow street, the bright September sun gently warm upon their faces.

They chatted and shared memories as they continued down the Barteljorisstraat, unaware for a moment that their afternoon walks would never be the same again. Casper noticed it first.

"What in the world is that, Corrie?" She looked as he pointed to a young couple crossing the street.

"I don't see what you mean, Father. What are you? . . ." She tried to get a good look at the man and woman without appearing rude. There was something different, but what was it?

"What's that they're wearing?" Father whispered. "On their coats. A yellow star."

"Yes. I see it now. And look—that man over there—he's got one, too." Corrie and Casper stopped for a moment, bewildered.

"I'll ask Mr. Weil. He'll know," Casper said, turning around. He started walking again, at a quicker pace, and Corrie hurried beside him.

Mr. Weil was standing in front of his fur shop, briskly washing the window. The cleaning cloth in his hand was a blur of white as he rubbed the window in furious circles.

"Excuse me, Mr. Weil," Casper began. "I was wondering. . ."

Mr. Weil spun around to face them, and the star on his coat jumped out at them in a flash of yellow. In big black letters the word "Jew" screamed its presence in the center of the star. Father and daughter tried to speak, but no words would come.

"Ah, ten Boom, it's only you," Mr. Weil spoke with relief. "I thought maybe—well, never mind. Did you want something? What's the matter? You two look as if you've had quite a shock." His large dark eyes searched their faces, then he realized they were staring at his coat.

"Oh, so that's it." He pointed to the yellow emblem. "This is the latest in fashion from the Nazi regime." His voice was strained with artificial humor. "Of course, it was designed exclusively for those who are Jewish." His sarcasm masked his pain, but Casper was not fooled. He took Mr. Weil's hand and held it for a long time, saying with his eyes all that could not be said with words. Corrie stood silently by, her vision blurred as tears filled her eyes. *Dear God. What does all this mean?*

"I really must be getting back to work."

Casper tipped his hat to the furrier and took his daughter gently by the arm to cross the street. Casper entered the watch shop, and Corrie closed the door carefully, wishing that by closing the door to the street, she could close out the heartache of the day. But Corrie knew that was impossible. As she sat at her desk, the strange yellow star would hang in her mind like an unwanted flag.

Several months later, the sound of marching men echoed through the Barteljorisstraat. Corrie looked out the front window of the shop and watched as a group of German soldiers broke into Mr. Weil's shop. They shoved Mr. Weil out of his store and proceeded to destroy the place.

Corrie's heart pounded as she quickly ran out the door and headed for Mr. Weil. She heard footsteps behind her, and in a flash Betsie was at her side. Together, they grabbed Mr. Weil and rushed him into the Beje. Casper joined the frightened trio in the dining room and spoke kindly to his neighbor.

"You are safe here with us, my friend. God will tell us what to do."

Mr. Weil looked up at Casper with fear in his eyes.

Corrie felt her heart begin to race. Suddenly the answer flew through her spirit like a swift, silent arrow.

"Willem will know what to do." She spoke the words with such confidence that she startled everyone.

Corrie left at once for Willem's home. Willem's son Kik answered Corrie's knock and ushered her into the kitchen where Tine was busy preparing lunch. Corrie greeted her sister-in-law with a hug and plunged into her story. Kik and Tine listened carefully but didn't seem to be at all shocked as Corrie related her hair-raising account of Mr. Weil and the soldiers.

"And so you see, I must speak with Willem right away," Corrie finished excitedly. She looked at Kik and Tine and wondered how they could remain so calm.

"Willem is not here right now," Tine replied, wiping the kitchen table with a soft blue rag. "Kik will take care of it for you."

Corrie stared in amazement at her tall young nephew.

"But what could you? . . ." Corrie started to protest, but Kik wrapped an arm around his flustered aunt.

"Don't you worry about a thing, Tante Corrie. You just listen to my directions and do exactly as I say. I will knock on the door in the alley tonight," Kik explained. "Before you open the door, make sure the hall light is off." He turned to his mother. "When Dad gets back, tell him I might not get back until tomorrow afternoon." Kik kissed his mother and

Corrie good-bye and was gone.

"What's the matter, Corrie?" Tine stopped her work for a moment and sat down at the table. "Kik is not a little boy anymore."

"But he's so young. How does he know what to do? His plan came to him so easily, you'd think he'd done this kind of thing many times before."

Tine said nothing but looked steadily at Corrie. Suddenly, Corrie realized what Tine's silence meant. Kik, Tine, Willem—they were all involved in the work of the Dutch underground! This illegal group of brave men and women did its best to sabotage the Nazi regime in Holland and help those who were special targets of the German army.

Corrie started to ask Tine a question, but Tine stopped her.

"The less you know, the better, Corrie. That is the policy of the underground movement. That way, if anyone is caught, they will not reveal any information the Gestapo is looking for. They can't stop us if they don't have any names to go on."

Tine patted Corrie's hand. "I think you'd better get back to the Beje. Mr. Weil must be ready to leave at nightfall."

As Corrie traveled back to Haarlem, she realized a plan was beginning to unfold. Corrie, Betsie, and Casper had crossed the line and entered into the underground simply by arranging things for Mr. Weil's safety. She sensed it was the Lord's plan and there was no turning back.

When the evening finally came and draped its darkness

around the city of Haarlem, the ten Booms welcomed its covering. A knock on the alley door signaled Kik's arrival, and the ten Booms gave him the precious life they had been sheltering there all day. Kik took Mr. Weil gently by the arm, and in a moment they were gone. Casper, Corrie, and Betsie stood in the darkened hall for a long time, praying that all would go well. They were now a link in the underground, and in the days to come, God's plan for saving lives would unfold before them in a tapestry of intrigue and danger.

In 1942, spring slipped into place without the usual stirrings of hope and new life. The Nazi leaders in Holland did their best to break the spirit of the people. More and more, the Dutch felt like caged animals. Curfew was now set at 8 P.M. It was no longer safe for young men to walk the streets during the day because Germany needed manpower for their ammunition factories. Without warning, soldiers would seize men on the streets and ship them off to Germany to work for the Nazis.

The word spread among the Jews of Haarlem that the ten Boom family on the Barteljorisstraat had helped a Jewish furrier escape from the Nazis. In a matter of weeks, young mothers with children, elderly couples, and middle-aged men appeared at the alley door of the Beje. All were desperate for shelter from the searching eyes of the Gestapo.

With help from Willem and his friends, Corrie organized the underground operation at the Beje. The ten Booms knew many people in Haarlem, and with the Lord's leading, they were able to enlist the help of many. One man was able to secure ration cards for the Jews; another man working with the phone company reconnected the Beje's phone. An electrical warning system was installed. Willem helped make contacts with people who lived in the countryside of Holland. Farms and homes away from the cities made the safest hiding places.

To protect the true identities of the people involved in the underground, all the workers went by the name Smit. When Kik took his Tante Corrie to a meeting of the national Dutch underground, Corrie met a Mr. Smit who would play a very important role in the operation on the Barteljorisstraat. This Mr. Smit would supervise the building of a secret room in the Beje.

Mr. Smit arrived at the Beje and inspected the odd old building.

"This is a marriage made in heaven!" he declared, referring to the two buildings that made up the Beje. He climbed the twisting stairwell to the third floor of the smaller building and inspected Corrie's bedroom.

"Take a good look at your room, Miss ten Boom. In one week you won't believe your eyes!"

The days that followed were busy ones at the Beje. At all hours of the day or night, men showed up at the door to work on the secret room. They used bricks to build the new wall, all of which had to be brought in a few at a time for safety's sake. Under Mr. Smit's direction, the brick wall was plastered and painted. He supervised the construction of a bookshelf that ran the length of the new wall.

Finally, the secret room was finished.

"What do you think?" Mr. Smit asked them. Corrie, Betsie, and Casper stared in astonishment at the room. It looked almost exactly as it had before, except for the bookshelves, but the bookshelves were obviously as old as the house!

Corrie peered at the new-old wall, vainly looking for a clue to where the entrance to the secret room was located. "I give up," she said to Mr. Smit. "Where is it?"

Mr. Smit laughed with pleasure as he kneeled down in front of the bookcase. He reached over to the left-hand corner at the bottom of the shelf and lifted up a two-foot square panel. "This is the gateway to safety."

"Superb job, Mr. Smit." A familiar voice sounded behind Corrie, and she turned to greet her brother.

"Willem, isn't this incredible?"

"It certainly is, Corrie." He shook hands with Mr. Smit, and together they walked down the stairs. The family gathered in the dining room while Betsie made a pot of tea.

Finished with his tea, Mr. Smit rose from his chair and bade the ten Booms good-bye. Willem and Corrie walked him to the door and thanked him for his help.

"This job of saving lives is the best job I have ever had," he said softly.

Corrie watched him leave, then turned to her brother with a question. "Who is that man?"

"He's an architect," Willem replied. "Perhaps one of the

best known in all of Europe."

"What's his name?" Corrie asked without thinking.

Willem looked at his sister and smiled. "Smit."

More and more Jews made their way to the refuge on the Barteljorisstraat; more and more were safely hidden away by the underground. In 1943, January's breath blew fiercely cold upon Holland and took its toll on the Dutch people. There was very little coal or wood available for burning, and some resorted to chopping down the trees in Haarlem for firewood. The winter dragged on, and hiding places in the country became scarce. It became clear that it would be necessary to use secret locations within the city.

By the summer of 1943, seven refugees (four men and three women) found a permanent hiding place in the Beje itself. Betsie planned activities and miniconcerts in the evening to help ease the boredom and fear of the fugitives. Together they became a close-knit family. Casper and his daughters did all they could to make their new friends feel at home in the Beje.

As the underground work increased, the risks increased as well. Corrie knew they were being watched, and once a neighbor warned her that the refugees living at the Beje were being too noisy. With Kik's help, they conducted drills with the warning buzzers until everyone could get to the secret room in under two minutes. Corrie knew it was only a matter of time before the Gestapo came down on them.

On February 28, 1944, a stranger appeared at the Beje asking for help for his Jewish wife. He needed money to get her out of town. Corrie arranged for him to receive the money that afternoon. After he left, Corrie headed for the stairs. She wasn't feeling well.

"Why Corrie, you've got a fever!" Betsie exclaimed, placing her hand on her sister's flushed face. "You must go to bed at once. I can tell by looking at you that you have the flu!"

"I can tell by the way I feel," Corrie mumbled. She fell into her bed with relief. Betsie pulled the covers over her, and in an instant she was asleep.

Something jerked Corrie awake. It was the sound of the warning buzzer. In a blur, people raced through her door and into the secret room, disappearing behind the wall. Corrie's heart fluttered wildly as she realized it was not a drill. The Nazis were at the Beje. The underground had been betrayed.

"Oh no," she moaned. "That man in the shop this morning!"

Seconds later the Nazis burst into Corrie's room.

"Where are you hiding them?"

"Hiding who? I don't know what you're talking about," Corrie said.

"Where is the secret room?" The Nazi yanked her to her feet.

"I don't know what you're talking about." Corrie's voice shook as she tried to dress herself as quickly as possible. All was quiet behind the wall.

"The captain will take care of you," he hissed as he shoved Corrie to the stairs. "He'll find out what it is you don't know!"

The Nazi agent prodded her back with the muzzle of his

revolver and took her down to the shop where the captain was waiting. Corrie's body ached, and the fever wrapped itself around her. The soldier left her with the captain. His eyes narrowed as he stared at Corrie. The ticking of the clocks hammered against Corrie's pounding head as she struggled to remain standing.

"So, you are the head of this little group, eh?" His voice cut sharply through the air. "Where is the secret room?"

"I don't know what you mean," she replied.

The captain slapped her face, and Corrie fell against the wall.

"Where are you hiding the Jews?"

"I don't know what you mean," she stammered.

The man began to beat her, and Corrie cried out to the Lord. At the name of Jesus, the man became enraged, but he stopped beating her.

He dragged her out of the shop and up to the dining room. Casper, Betsie, and Toos were there, and Corrie collapsed into a chair next to Betsie.

"Well, Captain?" the commander asked.

"She refuses to cooperate," he growled.

The commander pointed to Betsie. "See what you can do with her."

"Oh God, not Betsie!" Corrie moaned to herself. She looked at her father, and his blue eyes held her gaze for a moment. There was a strength in his eyes that calmed Corrie while the nightmare raged around her.

The captain returned with a bruised but silent Betsie.

The walls of the Beje shook as soldiers searched for the secret room. Silently, the four seated in the chairs prayed for the hidden Jews. Heavy footsteps echoed in the stairwell, and the search team approached their commander.

"We've torn the place apart, Sir. Their secret room must be invisible."

The commander grunted with disgust. "Never mind. We'll keep watch on the house until those Jews starve to death." His eyes glinted with satisfaction.

He's a madman, Corrie thought as she stared at the commander's face.

"Take them to the police station, along with the others."

"Others?" Corrie wondered as she looked around the dining room. "What others?"

The door to the parlor opened abruptly, and the stairwell creaked with footsteps as people descended the stairs. The soldiers directed everyone out the front door. Corrie gasped with horror as she saw Willem, Nollie, and Peter pass through the door to the shop. Casper, Betsie, Toos, and Corrie followed behind the rest of the group.

The winter sun blinded Corrie's eyes as she walked down the Barteljorisstraat to the police station. She held Casper's arm, and her mind filled with memories of the countless walks she had taken with her father. Haarlem's "Grand Old Man" dearly loved to walk its streets, but this was one walk Corrie wished her father did not have to take.

After having their names processed at the station, they were all herded back outside to a waiting bus. Corrie, her family, and fellow workers boarded the bus. As the bus began to move, Corrie pressed her face against the glass. "I don't know where we're going, Lord, but I know You do. Keep us in Your care."

Suddenly, she remembered the vision she had the first night the Germans had attacked Holland.

Corrie leaned over toward Betsie. "The dream!" she whispered.

"He knows, Corrie," she whispered. "He goes before us."

The bus arrived at Nazi headquarters, where the prisoners were questioned for hours. Then they were ordered into a large truck. The ten Booms huddled together as best they could, with Betsie and Corrie sitting on either side of their father. As the truck made its way along the dark roads, Corrie felt her head spinning with fever. Where were they going? What was going to happen next? The questions swirled around in her brain while she wrestled with the chilling arms of fear.

The truck rumbled to a stop in front of the federal prison at Scheveningen. It pulled into the prison yard, and the new captives were thrust into a large room with dusty yellow walls.

The female prisoners were ordered to leave the room.

Corrie, Betsie, Nollie, Toos, and the other women turned

from the places along the wall and followed the matron across the floor to a forbidding steel door. As Corrie walked past her father, her stomach knotted with the desire to run to him and hold him, to protect him from the horrors of prison.

"The Lord be with you, Father!"

"And also with you, my children." His face radiated the peace of Christ. "The best is yet to be."

With a slam of the door, Corrie lost sight of her father. She would never see him again on this earth.

The voice of a male guard shot across the room and jerked the women to attention. "The rest of you follow me."

One by one, the new women prisoners were put in their cells. Corrie watched as Nollie, Betsie, and Toos were shoved into different cells. Corrie was put into a cell number 384, alone and delirious with fever.

She fell onto the cot in the corner of her cell, and the fever took control of her. The evening stalked silently into the prison and underlined Corrie's loneliness in the solitary cell. No longer able to control her thoughts, memories swarmed around her and punished her already broken heart.

Nollie stood at the side of her cot.

Don't you like my hat, Corrie? Do you think Tante Jans will let me wear it to school? She'll probably say it's sinful! Nollie giggled and turned away. Corrie reached out for her but grasped only air.

"Must be hallucinating," she panted, struggling to sit up. "Musn't think about home."

"Corrie, my dear, do you think you could take a look at this watch? It's quite a difficult piece, but I know you can do it." Father ten Boom held the watch out to Corrie, and she strained to take it from him.

"I know you can do it, my dear!" He smiled at her, holding out the watch.

"Can't reach it, Poppa," she moaned. "Can't reach it."

"You are such a shrimp, Corrie!" Willem's young voice chimed in. *"I'll race you to the canal!"*

"Wait for me, Will!" Corrie called out to her brother.

"Silence!" A cold voice from behind the cell door cut through Corrie's feverish imaginings and for a moment slapped her back into reality. "Solitary prisoners will remain silent!"

Corrie lay back down, and in the silence that followed, tears flowed quietly down her cheeks. She wept until the dirty mattress was wet with her sorrow.

"I can't do it, Lord," she cried. "It's too much for me. I just can't."

When tears would no longer come, Corrie turned on her side and cupped her hands over her face. Empty of tears, she felt engulfed in the emptiness of her lonely cell. Then thoughts of home returned to penetrate the blackness, but this time they came on the wings of calmness and comfort. As Corrie felt her own hands on her face, she remembered how her father would tuck his children into bed each night. The last thing he would do was touch each child gently on the face, as if to say, "I love you and I'm watching over you."

The memory pushed aside the emptiness in her cell, and Corrie reached out for her heavenly Father. "Cover me, Lord," she prayed. "Hide me under the shelter of Your wings."

She fell asleep with His words on her lips.

The days at Scheveningen passed slowly, but Corrie sensed the presence of the Lord with her. She recovered from her illness, and as each day ended, she marked it down on the walls of her cell.

Sometimes, the loneliness and sheer boredom of her confinement loomed larger than life and threatened to sweep her into mindlessness. At times, she felt like a tiny dot on a black line that stretched on forever. But those were just feelings, she reminded herself. *We must walk by faith.*

Whenever it was possible, the prisoners communicated with one another by shouting through the openings of the doors. To Corrie's amazement and joy, she learned that almost everyone had been released from prison except for Betsie, Corrie, and Casper. She painfully wondered how her father was doing; she knew prison life would be too hard for an eighty-four-year-old man.

One day in April, the trap door on her cell door clanked open and in flew a letter. Corrie sat rooted on the cot for a few minutes, not believing what she was seeing. Finally, she picked it up. The return address was Nollie's.

Ripping open the letter, Corrie read it through a blur of tears. It was her first contact with home, and the "Dear Corrie" washed over her in a wave of love. There was good news:

Everyone was free except for Corrie and Betsie. Father was free, too, but his freedom was in walking with Jesus face-to-face. He lived only nine days after the arrest.

"I know this is hard news for you to bear," the letter continued, "but try and remember what Father always used to say—'The best is yet to be.' "

In May, Corrie was interrogated for four days by a Nazi lieutenant named Rahms. When asked who was involved in the underground, Corrie could only reply with the name "Smit." Instead of supplying him with information, she boldly witnessed to him about Christ.

On the fourth and final day of her hearings, the lieutenant brought out several papers and handed them to Corrie.

"What can you tell me about these papers?"

Corrie stared at the papers and recognized them immediately. The Gestapo must have found them in the Beje. There were lists of names, addresses, and specific details about the underground work. Corrie knew she was staring at her own death penalty.

"I can't explain them, Sir." Corrie's mind reeled with the thought that not only did those papers condemn her, they also condemned many of the people who worked with the underground.

The lieutenant took the papers from Corrie and walked toward the woodburning stove in his office. To Corrie's utmost surprise, he opened the door of the stove and shoved the papers in. Through silent tears of joy, Corrie watched the bright yellow flames devour the evidence.

Several days later, Corrie was summoned to the lieutenant's office again. Once inside his office, Corrie found herself surrounded by her family. She stared at them, not daring
to believe they were actually there.

"It is my imagination. I am only dreaming," she whispered.

"No, no, Corrie dear. We really are here!"

She looked up into Willem's eyes and collapsed in his
arms. Nollie, Betsie, Flip, and Tine gathered around her and
mingled their tears with hers. Corrie looked at each face and
marveled at God's grace.

"You look wonderful!" Nollie hugged Corrie again and
slipped something into Corrie's pocket. It was a tiny Bible.

"I will do all I can to get you and Betsie released,"
Lieutenant Rahms said quietly, "but I must warn you that it
is a next-to-impossible task."

Betsie and Corrie tearfully enjoyed the precious minutes
with their family and then reluctantly said good-bye. Corrie
was overjoyed with the treasure in her pocket—the Bible.
She prayed a prayer of heartfelt thanks to the shepherd Who
was so lovingly taking care of her. He had sent her His Word
to keep her and comfort her in those long, lonely days of
solitary confinement. Little did she know that her little Bible
would become a source of light not only for herself, but for
countless other women as well.

In June, all prisoners at Scheveningen were transferred
by train to Vught concentration camp in Holland.

CHAPTER 6

In Barracks #4 of Vught concentration camp, Betsie held Corrie's hand tightly.

"We are together, Corrie! I don't know what lies ahead, but we are together!" Corrie squeezed Betsie's hand in agreement. Together they would face whatever would come.

A stern-faced female guard marched into the barracks.

"Roll call is at 5 A.M. and 6 P.M. If anyone is late, roll call will be earlier. Today you will be assigned to work details." She turned to leave and then stopped for a moment. "The disobedient will pay for their disobedience."

The room was silent after she left. A guard ordered the prisoners to assemble in ranks of five in the main yard. Several officers walked up and down the rows of women, checking their lists and studying the women. The June sun felt warm on Corrie's face, and she squinted in the brightness. As the men consulted one another, a strange feeling swept over Corrie. *A slave market. I am in a slave market, waiting to be sold.*

Eventually, they called Corrie's name and assigned her to work in the Phillips factory where they assembled radios for German fighter planes. Mr. Moorman, the *Oberkapo* (prisoner in charge of the work detail), was a kind man who gave them a tour of the factory and explained what to do. Then he took Corrie to her bench.

"We must keep production up, or there will be trouble. However, they can't tell the difference between a good radio and a faulty one, so don't worry if you happen to connect the wrong wires." He looked at Corrie to see if she understood.

She smiled up at him. "I will do my best."

The workday at Vught was twelve hours long. When Corrie returned to the barracks, she found Betsie waiting at the door for her with bandaged hands.

"Betsie, what in the world happened?"

"They assigned me to the rope detail. You have to braid the ropes together." Betsie sighed and looked down at her hands. "The rope is very coarse, and I burned my hands raw on it."

Seeing the look of concern on Corrie's face, Betsie stopped and laid a bandaged hand on her sister's shoulder. "It's all right, Corrie. They've given me a new assignment. I am to stay right here in the barracks and sew prison uniforms with the other old ladies." She laughed. "That's what they call me, an old lady!"

The days at Vught passed quickly. The work was hard, and the lack of food took its toll on the prisoners. Betsie especially suffered from hunger, and her weight went down to ninety-six pounds. Every day, Corrie brought a portion of her lunch back to the barracks for Betsie. In the evenings, they read the Bible to all who would listen and shared the message of God's overwhelming love.

Roll calls were long, boring, and exhausting, and when the prisoners' performances were less than perfect, roll call was used as punishment. To stand at attention for an hour at a time racked the body with pain, but for Betsie and Corrie, roll call became an opportunity to see the wonder of creation. The August sun would go down with all the majesty of a royal procession. The reds and golds lit up the sky and scattered their brilliance over the yard of the camp, engulfing the prisoners in color. In the glow of those moments, Corrie and Betsie knew God was displaying a picture of His presence. It was a piece of glory, a reminder of God's kingdom that never fails. They felt every bit of pain as their muscles cried out for rest, but the display of their Lord's power ignited their hope in Him.

The men's camp at Vught was separated from the women's by a wall of barbed wire. During the lunch break at the factory, women would gather at the fence and try to get information about husbands and sons who were there. Others were fortunate enough to be working in the factories side by side with their loved ones. But happiness in Vught was a fragile thing: Often a wife would wait in vain for her husband to join her for the day. Daily, the piercing sound of gunshots in the men's camp grimly announced the death of more prisoners.

In September, the sound of bombs exploding in the distance kindled hope among the prisoners that the Allies were in

Holland. Maybe freedom was around the corner! Maybe the Germans were retreating! At the factory, Mr. Moorman explained that what they were hearing was actually the Germans destroying bridges. The Allies were coming, but they weren't in Holland yet.

All the women were ordered to return to their barracks.

In the men's camp, soldiers lined hundreds of prisoners up against the back wall and systematically shot them in their heads.

The next morning, the women and the surviving male prisoners were herded out of the camp. Corrie and Betsie marched together, their precious Bible hidden in Corrie's prison uniform. They arrived at the train tracks and were ordered to stand at attention. A freight train was waiting for its living cargo, the windowless boxcars forming a dreary line on the tracks. At a signal from the commander, the prisoners were ordered to climb into the boxcars. Soldiers pushed and prodded the people like cattle, until each car was stuffed with between eighty and one hundred prisoners.

The train jolted to a start several hours after it had been loaded. The stench in the boxcars became unbearable and the darkness overwhelming. Their destination was Germany. Slowly the engine pulled the living nightmare down the tracks for four days and four nights. It seemed to Corrie that the prince of hell himself must have masterminded this horrible exodus. She wondered if they would survive the trip. The train stopped and started several times, as if to prolong the agony. Finally, on the fourth day, it came to a full stop.

The doors were pulled open and the light of day blinded the prisoners as they poured out of the boxcars. Corrie squinted her eyes and saw a small lake near a grove of pine trees. In the distance there was a small town. A squad of soldiers directed the prisoners onto a road and ordered them to march. The lake borrowed its sparkle from the sun and shimmered in the morning light, unaware of the line of human misery that stumbled past its shores. One mile later, they arrived at Ravensbruck, the only all-women's concentration camp of Hitler's regime. Some women began to weep; Corrie looked over at her sister. Betsie grasped Corrie's hand and whispered the word "together." Together they walked on, clinging to the knowledge that they were not alone; their Savior walked with them through the gates of Ravensbruck.

For three days, the prisoners stood at attention in the camp's yard. At night, they slept on the ground. At the end of the third day, guards escorted the prisoners to the receiving building of the camp. Corrie panicked as she watched the women put all their belongings on the tables and take off their clothes to enter a large shower room. It would take a miracle to get the Bible past the guards. Corrie whispered a prayer.

"Corrie," Betsie groaned. "I. . .terrible cramps. . ."

Quickly grabbing Betsie before she could fall, Corrie asked a guard where the bathrooms were located.

"Bathrooms?" he asked scornfully. "What bathrooms? Use the shower room!" He led them to the shower room and left them there alone. Corrie looked around the room and saw the answer to her prayer. There was a stack of old furniture in the room. She pulled the Bible out from under her uniform and hid it behind the furniture.

They returned to the main room, undressed, and marched past the guards to the shower room. The water was cold, but it felt good as it washed away the dirt of many days. Corrie drew two prison dresses from a pile and gave one to Betsie. The dresses were worn thin, and when Corrie stuffed the Bible under her uniform, she knew it was hopeless. There was no human way she could conceal her secret from the guards.

"Lord, please hide me behind Your angels," she prayed desperately.

The women reentered the main room and Corrie watched as the guards searched each woman thoroughly, frisking them one by one. When it was Corrie's turn, she walked right past the guards. They did not even glance at her! Corrie's heart sang. *Aufseherinnen* (female guards) conducting a second round of searches pushed Corrie along past the second inspection. The Bible was safe!

The newcomers were sent to the quarantine block, where Corrie and Betsie were assigned to Barracks #8. They squeezed into a bed with three other women and fell asleep.

At 4 A.M., a whistle blew and awakened the prisoners for their morning ration of food. At 4:30, they assembled on the

Lagerstrasse, the broad street that ran the length of the camp. The women were organized in groups of one hundred each, ten women per row. At roll call, the guard counted the prisoners, checking and rechecking until the numbers coincided with the camp's official list. If anyone was missing, the others remained at attention until the missing were found. Latecomers were beaten without mercy.

Directly across from the quarantine barracks on the Lagerstrasse was the Strafblock. This was the punishment section of the barracks. The normal punishment was twenty-five lashes with a stick, but sometimes prisoners were sentenced to fifty to seventy-five blows. Day and night, screams of terror and utter despair filtered through the walls of the Strafblock.

In between roll calls, the new prisoners were ordered to their barracks. Corrie pulled out the Bible, and Betsie began to read to all who would listen. Each day the number of women who gathered together increased. God was searching for His children, and Corrie and Betsie held out His message to the condemned women of Ravensbruck. As the realities of the concentration camp worsened, the reality of God's presence became clearer and brighter.

In the middle of October, the new prisoners were transferred to permanent barracks. At the last row of buildings, at Barracks #28, the guard called out Prisoner 66729 and Prisoner 66730. Corrie and Betsie marched into their new quarters.

In the front part of the barracks was a large room with tables and benches where women sat knitting gray army socks. There were two rooms off the main room where the prisoners slept. A prison worker took Corrie and Betsie to their assigned room. "This room was built to accommodate two hundred women," said the worker. "But there are seven hundred living here now. Not to mention the millions of fleas," she added. Corrie groaned, but Betsie said, "Praise the Lord."

The large room was filled with wooden platforms three levels high. The platforms were grouped tightly together with only a few narrow aisles making a way to get through the room. Corrie and Betsie's bunk was on the second tier in the middle of an island of platforms. They had to climb up and crawl over several bunks to get to their own.

At six o'clock, the whistle sounded for the evening roll call, and Betsie and Corrie made their way to the Lagerstrasse. They took their places with the other women of Barracks #28. The newcomers couldn't take their eyes off the women of Ravensbruck who stood around them. Their bodies were wasted away, their skin deformed with running sores. But the thing that scared Corrie the most was the look on their faces—they stared straight ahead, their eyes glazed over with despair. Death was written on their faces.

"Help us to bring them Your hope," Corrie prayed silently.

The following day, after roll call, the prisoners were assigned to their work details. A nearby factory paid the Nazis for laborers, and every day thousands of women marched to the factory and reported for work. Corrie and Betsie's first assignment was with the Siemens factory. Located south of the camp next to the railroad tracks, the plant's work consisted of dragging heavy pieces of metal from railroad cars to the factory building. After eleven hours of exhausting labor, the women marched back to the camp, engulfed once again by the gray concrete walls of Ravensbruck.

In the evening, the ten Boom sisters started their Bible studies in Barracks #28. Women gathered around one of the few lights in the huge room—women from all over Europe and of all denominations. They would sing quietly and then the Bible would be read. Corrie breathed a prayer of thanks that her father had taught them German. Many of the women understood German, and for those who did not, others would translate the reading for them. Each night more women joined the group.

"I can't understand why the guards never come in here," Corrie said to Betsie one evening as they climbed over the bunks to get to bed. "Not once have they come in to inspect the place. It's amazing." Corrie settled down in the straw and scratched one of her countless flea bites.

"I know why they don't come in here," Betsie replied. Corrie could tell by the tone of Betsie's voice that she was smiling in the darkness. "I discovered the reason today. The guards refuse to come in because of the fleas!" Betsie laughed. "Fleas, Cornelia ten Boom. Because of the fleas, we can freely share the gospel with our fellow prisoners."

In November, Corrie and Betsie's work assignment was changed: They now worked within the camp, digging up uneven patches of ground and smoothing them out with huge metal rollers. The digging took its toll on Betsie. Each day she weakened, until she could hardly carry her shovel. A guard who accused Betsie of being lazy whipped her until she bled.

When it was clear that Betsie could no longer do manual labor, she was assigned to the knitting detail in the barracks. Corrie managed to get her assignment changed and joined her sister in Barracks #28. Together Corrie and Betsie spent their workdays knitting socks and sharing the news of God's love with their fellow knitters. Women who were sick or weak were assigned to the knitting detail, and the ten Boom sisters often had the privilege of seeing women pass through the gates of death with the name of Christ on their lips.

December winds blew coldly upon the camp and roll call became more torturous than ever. In an effort to keep warm, the women stamped their feet on the snowy ground. To Corrie, the pounding of the thirty-seven thousand women's feet sounded like a death march. Betsie's legs grew weaker, and Corrie noticed she was beginning to cough. Unable to endure the cold and the hunger, some women were dying during roll call.

One night in the barracks, Betsie had something important to tell Corrie. Corrie studied Betsie's thin face. Her cheeks were sunken, and there were dark circles under her eyes.

"What is it, Betsie?"

"The Lord has shown me what we are to do after we get out of here."

"You mean we will be released? Are you sure?"

"Oh yes, it is quite clear. We will have a house in Holland for rehabilitation. People who have suffered in the concentration camps will need to recover before they can again have normal lives.

"The house is very large—a mansion really—with lots of windows and shiny wood floors. There's a large yard with many gardens where the people can grow flowers and vegetables."

"When, Betsie? When will this happen?"

"We will be free before the new year comes. . . . And what a staircase! It's such a marvelous, wide staircase. And there are statues, you know, in the front hall."

Betsie continued, "And after the war, we are going to have a concentration camp."

"What?" Corrie said loudly. She sat up and bumped her head on the bunk above her.

"Shh. You'll wake everybody up. The camp is in

Germany. They need so desperately to learn how to love."

Corrie lay back down and thought about the *Aufseherin-nen* and the S.S. men—special police who served the Nazi party.

"Only God could teach them how to love," she muttered.

"We must tell them. We must tell everyone that no pit is so deep that God is not deeper still." Her voice grew weaker. "And we must paint the camp with bright colors and plant flowers."

The next morning when the whistle blew for roll call, Betsie could not move. She was carried to the camp hospital where she died.

Corrie doubled over, sobbing. "It can't be," she wept. "It can't be!"

Corrie began to walk around the camp in a daze, stumbling on the snowy streets. She heard footsteps running, and someone grabbed her from behind.

It was a woman named Mien. "You've got to come."

"I don't want to see her. I know she's dead."

"You've got to see her, Corrie. I know a way to get in without anyone seeing us. Come on."

Mien took her to a window in the back of the hospital.

"They put the bodies in the washroom." She lifted up the window. "Climb in."

Corrie hesitated, but Mien insisted she go in. She lowered herself into the room and covered her eyes with her hands. A line of starved bodies lay on the floor.

"Look, Corrie! Look at her!"

Corrie looked down at Betsie, expecting to see her thin sister. What she did see took her breath away. Betsie was beautiful. Every trace of suffering had disappeared; her face was full and clear, as if she had never been starved or ill.

"It's a miracle," Mien whispered.

Corrie nodded wordlessly as she stared at her sister.

Betsie was free.

A few days later, Prisoner 66730 was called out of her line.

"Stand at the head of the line."

Other women were ordered to join Corrie, and they waited for roll call to end. The wind was especially cold that day, and Corrie felt her legs and feet beginning to swell. She could see the smoke from the cremation ovens rise above the camp. Perhaps it was her turn to die.

Corrie shuddered in the cold and committed herself to the Lord. Roll call continued for three hours, and Corrie used that time to tell a young girl next to her about Christ. The girl listened carefully and then asked the Savior to come into her life.

Finally, roll call ended, and Corrie was ordered to report to the administration offices. An officer called her name and handed Corrie a piece of paper. She stared down at it, afraid to believe what she was seeing. It was a certificate of discharge! She was not going to die, after all. She was going to live!

Corrie shuffled from one desk to the next one. Another officer gave her a pass for the train, then she was directed to a room where medical inspections were taking place. Sharp pains shot up and down her legs and ankles as she waited in the line. The doctor took one look at her legs and ordered her to the hospital.

"They'll let you out if the swelling goes down."

Corrie stayed in the hospital for seven days. The days passed slowly and were filled with horror as Corrie witnessed the cruelty of the nurses there. Many of the women were dying, begging for water, but the nurses would only laugh and make fun of them. Some prisoners fell out of their beds, unable to move, and were left on the floor to die.

On the seventh day, Corrie passed the physical and was given civilian clothes and a coat, then ordered to put her signature on a paper that stated she had never been ill-treated at Ravensbruck. She signed the useless piece of paper.

"Report to the gate," an S.S. man snarled.

As Corrie waited at the gate with a small group of women, someone from Barracks #28 approached her.

"Corrie," she whispered, "that girl you witnessed to at your last roll call died today. She spoke to me about you. I thought you would want to know."

The girl scurried away at the sound of a soldier's boots. The guard pushed open the iron gates and an *Aufseherin* gave the command to follow. Corrie felt like she was dreaming as she passed through the gates. She saw the lake, pine trees still gracing its shores. The steeple of a church in the nearby town was pointing to heaven. Heaven. Poppa was there, and Betsie, and many other women who had been introduced to Christ at Ravensbruck. Corrie breathed a prayer of thanks. She had left her Bible with one of the women, and she hoped that many more would find eternal life in its pages.

The *Aufseherin* led the ex-prisoners to the train station and left them there. It seemed odd to Corrie that she was free, and the *Aufseherin* was returning to prison. Corrie reached Berlin on New Year's Day. One week later, at Ravensbruck, all women in Corrie's age group were killed. Corrie had been released by mistake.

At the huge train station in Berlin, Corrie boarded the train headed for Holland. After three days of traveling, the train crossed the border of her homeland and pulled into the station at Groningen. Corrie made her way to the hospital there. She was exhausted, and her legs ached. She hadn't eaten since she left Ravensbruck. Once she was inside the hospital, the nurses fed her, made up a bed for her, then led her to a room with a white tub filled with clean, warm water.

The nurse closed the door behind her, and Corrie lowered herself into the tub. Her ravaged skin welcomed the healing warmth of the water, and Corrie cried for joy. She was free. She was really free.

Ten days later, Corrie was at Hilversum, weeping in her brother's arms. Tine hovered around her like a mother hen and insisted that she stay at least two weeks with them. In the days that followed, Corrie told them about Ravensbruck, about Betsie's shining life, and the miracle at her death. Willem told Corrie the news about Kik, who had been arrested and sent to Germany. They did not know if he was dead or alive.

Corrie wanted to go home to the Beje. Willem arranged the trip, and a friend drove her to Haarlem.

But something had changed. Corrie had learned that God alone was her home. As much as she loved the Beje, she knew she couldn't stay. Betsie often said the safest place to be was in the center of God's will, and Corrie knew what His will for her was. She must tell everyone she could that no darkness can overcome the light of God's love.

Early in May 1945, Holland was liberated by the Allies, and the country rejoiced in its freedom. Corrie went from church to church and home to home, sharing with people what she and Betsie had learned in Ravensbruck. After one meeting, a woman offered her home to Corrie for the rehabilitation work Betsie had spoken of in Ravensbruck.

Corrie accompanied the woman to her home, and as

she looked up at the large windows and the surrounding gardens, she could almost hear Betsie's voice. "It's a mansion, really. . . ." Her shoes squeaked on the shiny wood floors, and she studied the statues set into the walls, trying not to cry as she climbed the grand staircase.

The Lord opened doors for Corrie all over Europe, and she faithfully carried the message of His love to all who would listen. Often, she would lay a map out on her bed and ask the Lord where He wanted her to go next. Sensitive to the Spirit's leading, she would go where He said to go.

She made her first trip to America where for almost a year she proclaimed the gospel. She preached the gospel wherever she could, but she especially enjoyed going to the prisons to share her story. From Sing Sing to San Quentin, Corrie spoke of the power of God's love. Sometimes before she began to speak, the prisoners would disrupt the meeting with jeers and yells. What did that old lady have to say to them? Then Corrie would begin talking about her prison term, and everyone would become quiet. She knew how they felt, and she gave them the key to inner freedom—Jesus Christ.

As her time in America came to an end, Corrie knew in her heart that the Lord was ready to send her to a place she did not want to go: Germany. *Surely I have suffered enough, Lord,* she thought. *Don't send me back to that terrible place.* But the Lord insisted, and Corrie submitted to His will.

Corrie arrived in Germany and was overwhelmed by the

needs that stretched out before her. Millions of Germans were homeless; millions were in despair over the evils wrought by Adolf Hitler. People had set up homes wherever they could; Corrie discovered a factory crowded with people. She decided she would live with them and try to reach them for the Lord. The living conditions were crowded and the air laced with horrible smells, but Corrie was used to that. She lived out her faith among the people and pointed them to Christ.

While in Germany, Corrie began to see more of Betsie's vision come to pass. A man from a relief organization offered her the use of a concentration camp in Darmstadt for her rehabilitation work. The gray barracks were painted green, and Corrie smiled at the thought of her sister's dream.

How wonderful to be in the hands of the living God, she thought. *It is the adventure of a lifetime.*

More than once, Corrie saw a guard or a nurse from Ravensbruck. Each time, she remembered their cruelty and found it impossible to forgive them. She prayed desperately for the Lord to give her His love for them, and He always answered that prayer. In His strength, she forgave, and as she shook the hand of one ex-guard, the love of God poured through Corrie in a powerful wave of love.

Corrie followed her Lord wherever He led her. She traveled to over sixty countries and preached to all kinds of people from all walks of life. She told the story of surviving Ravensbruck, where over ninety-five thousand women lost their lives. Corrie's release was no mistake; it was the hand of her Lord directing her path and unveiling His plan. She learned that when all seems lost, Jesus remains, and the best is yet to be.

In her travels, Corrie discovered that the needs of man are the same all over. All people need the Savior, and many are ignorant of His love and how well He provides for His people. As she observed the empty hearts of men and women, she was reminded of a little boy in her Bible class for mentally challenged children. Corrie was telling the class about the feeding of the five thousand, and little Carl was totally engrossed in the story. Suddenly, he leaped out of his seat, crying enthusiastically: "There is plenty! There is plenty! Take as much as you want!"

Corrie wished people could see God's love and care for them as clearly as Carl had.

Corrie told the story of the war years in her book *The Hiding Place.* It became a best-seller, and World Wide Pictures made a film based on Corrie's book. One day, while the film was being made, Corrie watched as the woman who played her came through the gates of Ravensbruck. The impact of her suffering swept over Corrie; she remembered the pain, the loss of her sister and her father. She wept openly, and as she wept, the Lord healed Corrie's deep hurt. She realized her suffering had paved the way for her to preach the good news: There is no pit so deep that God is not deeper still.

Corrie ten Boom continued to serve the Lord well into

her eighties. In 1977, Corrie settled in California in a home she named "Shalom House." She was no longer able to travel all over the world as she had been doing for so many years; her heart was weakening. But despite the obstacles of a weak body, she had tremendous drive and energy that enabled her to accomplish goals she set for herself with the leading of the Lord.

Corrie was writing books and making films to bring people to know Jesus when, at the age of eighty-six, she suffered a stroke that paralyzed her right side and took away her ability to speak. The paralysis eventually disappeared, but she never regained the ability to speak aloud. This, however, did not stop her from communicating. Her companion, Pamela Rosewell, the housekeeper, and Lotte, a close friend of Corrie's, managed to understand Corrie's desires and thoughts by asking her questions that Corrie could answer by signaling yes or no.

Lotte helped her finish another devotional book, and Corrie received visitors to Shalom House, ministering without words but with her eyes and her smile. She enjoyed the garden in the backyard and often walked outside, enjoying the flowers and the sky. No doubt she was often reminded of her mother's and Betsie's love for flowers and the blue sky.

Corrie submitted to the Lord at this difficult time of not being able to speak freely. There were tears of frustration at times, but she never rebelled in anger against her Lord. In 1979, Corrie suffered another stroke: This one left her incapable of walking. She could sit up in a wheelchair, however, and so her tour of the garden was done by chair, with a friend pushing gently from behind. She could understand and communicate with a nod or a simple yes. It was difficult for those who loved her to see her so confined, but they marveled at Corrie's peace in the midst of such suffering.

In the fall of 1980, Corrie suffered her final stroke. She survived the stroke but was no longer able to sit in her wheelchair. She was extremely weak, and her friends could see in her eyes a deep desire to go home to be with her Lord. However, the days continued to stretch out before her, and once again those who cared for her were amazed at Corrie's surrender to her Father's will. For some reason, God chose to have her live for two and a half more years, silent and unable to move from her bed.

God's plans are never wasteful, but fruitful. In the past, Corrie's mother, her voice silenced and her body still because of a stroke, had managed to minister to others through the prayer in her heart and the love that shone in her eyes. Now Corrie did the same. God's love flowed through her to those who lived with her and those who came to see her at her home. People literally experienced Christ's love and Christ's presence in Corrie. She witnessed silently to the fact that our peace, joy, and fulfillment come not from what we can do in life for God, but from God Himself.

Thirty-nine years before, while in solitary confinement in Scheveningen Prison, Corrie had written to her sister Nollie about God's timing:

Once I asked to be freed but the Lord said, "My grace is sufficient for you." I am continually looking at Him and trying not to be impatient. I won't be here one minute longer than God deems necessary. Pray for me that I can wait for His timing.*

Now Corrie patiently and joyfully waited for her freedom from the prison of her body, and when the day came, she was ready.

On her birthday, April 15, 1983, Corrie walked through the gates of her Father's heaven into His glory. No doubt there was a great celebration that day in heaven.

Corrie's path took her to many places. She always called herself a "tramp for the Lord." From a concentration camp to foreign palaces, Corrie told the eternal story of God's love for all people. Her journey ended in the unveiled presence of her Lord, face-to-face.

---

*Corrie ten Boom. *Prison Letters* (Old Tappan, N.J.: Fleming H. Revell Company, 1975).

ERIC LIDDELL

OLYMPIAN AND MISSIONARY

by Ellen Caughey

CHAPTER 1

Stoke-on-Trent, England, July 1923

The runners were lining up in their positions on the cinder track. Although no lines were drawn to show them where to be, these men had been in enough races to give each other the space they needed.

At least for the moment.

Twenty-one-year-old Eric Liddell of Scotland, known as "The Flying Scotsman," had received a good position just one spot to the right of the most inside "lane." All runners wanted that inside position, especially during the race. Whoever ran there didn't have to run as far, for one thing. And if no one was ahead of you, you would likely win the race.

To win this race meant a lot. The winner today would earn a place on Great Britain's Olympic team and the chance to race in Paris next summer.

Eric glanced to his right and smiled. He knew by name all the runners here: men from England, Scotland, and Ireland, including the man tying his shoes next to him. J. J. Gillies was one of England's best runners, and the favorite to win this 440-yard race. Earlier that day Eric had won the 100- and 220-yard races. No one expected him to win three races on the same day.

As he did with all the runners in every race, Eric offered his hand to J. J. and shook it. But instead of saying "Good luck," Eric said, "Best wishes for the race." Eric didn't believe in luck. To him, all things happened for a reason.

Reaching into his coat pocket for a small shovel, Eric then returned to his starting place. Carefully, he carved out of the cinder track two small holes, just the size of the toes of his shoes.

When the race began, Eric would need these holes to help "launch" himself into the race. Most runners brought their own shovels to races. They had practiced carving just the right-sized holes—not too big and not too small—so they could get their best start.

Then, as the runners began to take off their coats and long pants, the race official walked toward the track. Clearing his throat, he proclaimed, "Runners, take your marks!"

Eric felt his heart start to beat faster as he crouched down and placed the toes of his shoes in the holes. He knew that he was a poor starter, and that he would have to run as hard as he could to finish in the top three.

But he would never have a start quite like this!

Out of the corner of his eye, Eric could see J. J. Gillies. J. J. was looking at that inside lane, bordered by a wooden railing. As the seconds ticked by, J. J.'s eyes became like slits. *J. J. is determined to win,* Eric thought. *Are my legs strong enough to give him a race?*

With the small starting pistol in hand, the official raised his arm toward the sky. "On the count of three, gentlemen, and then the gun will sound." Seconds seemed like minutes to the racers until the official spoke again. "One, two, three. . ." *bang!*

The runners' arched bodies exploded forward until they straightened, their legs and arms making them go faster and faster.

Fifteen yards into the race, J. J. Gillies made his move, the move he had plotted in his head minutes earlier. But instead of waiting for an opening, J. J. cut right in front of Eric!

In a second, Eric felt himself lose his balance and go flying into the wooden railing—and then roll over two times onto the grass. Eric sat up and shook himself, then blinked his eyes. Across the track someone was calling his name. Then another voice demanded his attention.

"Get up, get up!" yelled two race officials, waving their arms wildly. "You're still in the race!"

Eric couldn't believe it. But he didn't have time to ask why. Scrambling to his feet, he hurdled the railing onto the track. By this time, even the slowest runner was twenty yards ahead of him. *There is no way,* Eric thought, *unless it is God's will.*

And then Eric started running.

First, Eric began swinging his arms so they looked like two very active windmills. Then his fists started punching the air in front of him, as if the air were holding him back.

When his legs really started moving, Eric raised his knees high, as if he were leading a marching band. And finally, to make himself go even faster, Eric threw back his head, his chin up, his eyes looking to the sky.

Yard after yard, Eric began to catch the pack of runners. His arms punching him forward even harder, Eric, to the amazement of the crowd, was now in fourth place. But he was still ten yards behind the leader, J. J. Gillies.

Even though Eric was from Scotland, and was most loudly cheered by Scots, now everyone started cheering and shouting his name. Few spectators could believe what they were seeing.

"Forty yards to go, Liddell!" one man shouted to Eric as he overtook the third-place runner. Forty yards, two runners to pass. He couldn't feel his arms or his legs. He could barely take a breath. Forty yards seemed like forty miles to him. But he would not stop.

Again, he willed his hands to punch harder, his knees to lift higher, his arms to swing faster. As he neared the finish line, Eric threw his chest out and his head back one more time—and passed J. J. Gillies to win the race. Eric Liddell had won the 440-yard race by two whole yards.

Eric had used everything he had to win the race. He fell to the ground, gasping for breath, and soon found himself surrounded by the crowd. There were race officials, college friends, reporters and photographers from the local newspapers, and even children.

Eric could only nod or smile at their questions. They were already asking him about the Olympics, about his training program, about his next race. Did he know J. J. Gillies before? What would he say to him when he saw him? Everyone could see that Gillies had pushed him off the track.

And then a young voice caught his attention.

"Sir, how did you learn to run so fast?"

Eric closed his eyes, and a curious expression came over his face. Instead of the endless blue sky, all he saw in his mind were gray stone buildings and matching gray skies. All he could feel was the sadness of the six year old that he had been. A boy who didn't know how to run. A boy very far away from home.

London, England, September 1909

Eric felt his brother nudge him forward ever so slightly. But his shoes felt nailed to the floor, and his eyes seemed stuck on his shoes! Again, but with greater force, Robbie tried to edge Eric closer to the massive wooden desk at the front of the room—the desk of the headmaster, W. B. Hayward.

As Eric raised his blond head slowly and somehow managed to look straight ahead, he spied a pair of kindly old eyes set in a wrinkled face, a face that reminded him of his grandfather. At once, Mr. Hayward arose and offered his hand to both boys.

"Welcome to the School for the Sons of Missionaries,

young men! Did you have a good first night here?"

Eric and Robbie looked at each other and then at the floor. Last night was unlike any night they had ever spent—but surely the headmaster knew that.

All new students entering the boarding school had to undergo an "initiation," or a time of testing that the other students had made up. In 1909 at the School for the Sons of Missionaries, the initiation went like this: The older students lined up in two rows, facing each other, with each boy holding a knotted handkerchief. As Eric and Robbie ran between the lines, they were swatted with the handkerchiefs.

Eric and Robbie could hardly wait to get back to the room they shared after that. "It wasn't so bad, was it, Eric?" Robbie had said last night. But Eric hadn't wanted to talk much. "Is it Mother, then?" At age eight, Robbie, a sandy-haired older version of his brother, always wanted to make Eric feel better.

On his metal bed, six-year-old Eric tried to curl up into a smaller and smaller ball.

Eric knew it would only be seconds before Robbie came over to see if he was crying. Sure enough, soon he could hear the padding of his brother's feet crossing the small room. And then he felt his brother's breath against his cheek. "Eric, talk to me. Please."

Slowly, Eric turned to face his brother and his best friend, his dimpled chin quivering. But he said nothing.

"You know, we will have to get used to this. And we will

have to pretend when we see Mother that everything is fine."

Eric swallowed loudly. "Do Mother and Jenny have to go back to China?"

Robbie nodded. "You know they do. That's where Father is."

Closing his eyes, Eric thought he heard Robbie say good night, even though it had not been a good one at all. He couldn't imagine any night away from his family ever being good.

Headmaster Hayward looked the Liddell brothers up and down, from the tops of their sandy blond heads to the laces on their worn leather shoes. *Robert, or Robbie as he wants to be called, seems so much healthier than poor little Eric,* he thought to himself. *I must do something about this Eric, yes, I must. No six year old should look so pale and so thin! Makes one wonder what life was like in China. . . .*

As if aware of the headmaster's thoughts, Eric and Robbie again gave the floor their most careful attention. But at the sound of the older man clearing his throat, both heads shot up.

"I trust this will be a good first term for you both," Mr. Hayward said. "Besides your usual classes, you'll be learning to play rugby. . .er, rugger, I think the boys call it. Great sport, rugby! Sure to bring out the apples in your cheeks!"

In the month that followed, "rugger" became a favorite sport of both Robbie and Eric, one that they learned quickly. Although rugby is sometimes called "rugby football," the sport is very different from American football. Using an oval-shaped ball—a ball that can be easily bounced and kicked—fifteen-player teams attempt to score a try by moving, kicking, or passing the ball down the field and across a certain line. There is no blocking or tackling in rugby, and no player on a team may run ahead of the ball down the field.

Sometimes they would have as many as three or four games a week, and many practices in between. And because there are no time-outs allowed in rugby, Eric was becoming stronger and stronger, a fact observed by the old headmaster.

"You must be liking the breakfast porridge, young man," Mr. Hayward greeted Eric one day as he left the rugby field.

Eric's blue eyes sparkled, and he laughed loudly. The headmaster couldn't help but notice that the boy's cheeks looked as if they were painted with pink roses. "Yes, Sir," he finally answered.

"Or maybe it's the meat pudding?" the man continued, knowing exactly how most boys felt about that often-served dinner dish.

Eric shook his head wildly, and then ran off as the headmaster shooed him away. *Who would have imagined a few weeks ago,* the headmaster thought, shaking his head. *And it looks as if the boy can run, too!*

During Eric and Robbie's first month at the School for the Sons of Missionaries, their mother, Mary Liddell, had stayed nearby in an apartment just to make sure that her sons were liking school. Now, as the time came for her to return to China to join her husband, she made a final trip to the school.

The occasion was a rugby game, and as most of the boys' parents were serving as missionaries overseas, Mary would be one of the few parents there. Because she didn't want to upset Eric and Robbie, she stayed in the headmaster's office until the game began and then went to the playing field.

She had to see her sons one last time. She had to know they would be all right without her.

There were Eric and Robbie, along with the other rugby forwards, laughing and holding on to each other's shoulders as they tried to kick the ball to the players behind them, signaling the official start of the game. The boys were concentrating so hard that they never saw their mother. Mary smiled and turned away, pleased.

She didn't want to think about the next time she would see Robbie and Eric. She knew it would be years from now. *God will take care of them,* she told herself. *God will hear my prayers and the prayers of my sons.*

That night as Mary and Jenny boarded a steamer ship for China, Eric cried himself to sleep in his little bed. He had waited until Robbie went to sleep; he did not want Robbie to know.

Someday I'll go back, too, Eric promised himself. *Someday Father and I will work together in China.* And then, finally drifting off to sleep, Eric tried to remember just what China was like.

CHAPTER 2

Siaochang, China, 1906

"Yellee! Yellee!"

Eric crouched down lower in his hiding spot as he heard the quick, soft footfalls of platform shoes coming closer. He and Robbie loved to play games with their amah, and hide-and-seek was one of their favorites. As he heard his Chinese nanny call his name—she could not say "Eric" so she called him "Yellee"—he started to laugh excitedly.

And then her face met his under the table. "There you are, Yellee," the amah said to Eric in Chinese, tugging at his Chinese-style quilted coat. Laughing herself, she pulled him out and plopped him on her lap. "Enough games for now. It's time for your lessons with Lordie and Jiernie."

Trying not to smile, Eric imagined that "Lordie" and "Jiernie"—Robbie and Jenny—had picked their own hiding places by now. None of them was eager to be in school.

Tagging along obediently, Eric followed his amah to one of the two schools in the mission "compound." One school was for boys, and the other was for girls. In China at this time, only boys were given an education. But when the Christian missionaries arrived, they insisted that girls attend school, too.

Surrounded by a high wall made of hardened mud, the compound at Siaochang where Eric and his family lived consisted of four large brick houses, the schools, a hospital, and a chapel for church services. The village of Siaochang, which included the mission compound, consisted of small houses made of mud and another high mud wall, as well as a gate.

The gate remained open during the day. But when night came, the gate was closed and locked. Now there was peace in China—but for years the people of Siaochang had feared for their lives.

Eric, Robbie, and Jenny loved to hear their mother and father tell them stories of what China was like when they first arrived. During the winters at Siaochang, when they spent most of their time indoors, their parents would first read to them from the Bible—and then continue their stories from the night before, stories that usually ended at a very exciting part.

After the Reverend James Liddell had arrived in Shanghai, China, in 1898, and Mary Liddell in 1899, they traveled to Mongolia, a northern province of China, to set up a mission station there. Mongolia! The name alone was enough to send shivers up one's spine. It brought to mind jagged, forbidding mountain ranges, never ending deserts, and wild, roaming peoples.

But there was trouble brewing all over China. A secret group called the Boxers had been organized, a group dedicated to killing all foreigners in China, and especially Christians. The Boxers, who got their name because they made karate-style slashes in the air, believed that Christian foreigners were the reason many Chinese had lost their jobs. Because they believed their bodies could stop bullets and even cannonballs, no foreigner could fight them and win.

At first the Boxers took their message of hate and violence to the countryside, not the big cities. In the country they would tell the poor people of China—the peasants—that if they did not do as they said, they would lose their crops because no rain would fall. The peasants were very superstitious, and they believed the Boxers.

Six months after James and Mary arrived, the Boxers attacked Mongolia!

In the middle of the night, James and Mary grabbed one small suitcase and rode in a rickety old wagon driven by a mule for many miles. When, after several days, they reached the seacoast, they boarded a boat and sailed once again for Shanghai. But not all Christian missionaries were so fortunate. More than two hundred were killed by the Boxers before the secret group was overthrown.

Shortly after Eric was born and Robbie was two years old, James received his new assignment in Siaochang, a village lying in the Great Plain of northern China, a region known for its extreme temperatures. Siaochang was one of two mission stations in the Great Plain, an area of more than ten million people (mostly farmers) and ten thousand villages. Eric and Robbie, and later Jenny, were the only children in Siaochang who weren't Chinese!

At school, the Liddell children were learning the Chinese language, as well as other subjects. Compared to the English alphabet, which has twenty-six letters, the Chinese language, known as *kwan hwa,* has fifty thousand characters or letters. Even to write a simple sentence, Chinese children must learn three thousand characters, or *wen hwa.* For Eric, going to school with his amah meant learning more and more of these strange symbols.

After school, Eric played with his many Chinese friends. He learned how to play Ping-Pong and chess, he learned to use chopsticks to eat, and he learned many Chinese songs. The people of Siaochang were always singing, whether out in the wheat fields or in their mud houses at night.

Summer 1906 was the last summer Eric would spend in China for awhile. The next year James would be returning home to Scotland for what missionaries called a "furlough," or a vacation.

That summer was spent like all the other summers Eric could remember. To escape the intense heat of Siaochang, where temperatures would reach 100 degrees Fahrenheit on most days, the Liddells traveled east to the coast, to the town of Pei-tai-ho on the Gulf of Pei-chili.

Dressed in his one-piece bathing suit held up by shoulder straps, Eric spent his days on the beach, splashing and laughing in the warm water and taking swimming lessons from Mary. In August, James Liddell could join his family because that was the time of year for the harvest in Siaochang. People spent time out in the fields and not in church.

News traveled slowly to China in those days, but that didn't bother James Liddell. As he read a prized newspaper from home, he couldn't wait to tell his family the biggest news from Scotland.

"Mary, you simply won't believe this!" James exclaimed, rubbing his graying mustache.

"Father, may I see, too?" Robbie asked, not wanting to be left out. Eric peered over his brother's shoulder, trying to see what had captured his father's attention.

"Wyndham Halswelle! What a name, what a story for Scotland!"

James was greeted by looks of disbelief. "Whozawell?" Eric imitated.

Laughing, James explained. "He's the first Scot to win a medal in track at the Olympics, Eric. You know the Olympics? The international sports competition held every four years?" The boys' faces were blank, but James continued anyway. "Well, Halswelle won the silver medal for second place in the 400-meter race."

"Then that means no Scot has ever won first place, right, Father?"

Smiling at Eric's understanding, James nodded. "That's right, Son. No Scottish runner has ever won the Olympic gold medal." Thinking a moment, James realized that he didn't want to give Eric the wrong message. He had been happy for this runner because he was from Scotland. But winning a medal at the Olympics wasn't everything.

"Eric, winning a medal isn't that important. What matters is how you run the race—of life. Do you remember what Paul wrote to the church at Corinth?" Reaching on the sand for his ever present Bible, James flipped the pages to the New Testament. "His idea was: 'Run in such a way to get the prize.' And what prize is that?"

Eric's blue eyes didn't blink. "The prize of heaven, Father."

CHAPTER 3

London, England, 1912–1920

The School for the Sons of Missionaries was a small school, with no more than 150 students in all. But even so, the boys were outgrowing the gray stone buildings of Eric's earliest memory, and headmaster W. B. Hayward went looking for a bigger "campus."

In 1912, as the Royal Naval School, also in London, moved to a larger complex, the School for the Sons of Missionaries moved into the navy's buildings. Eric and Robbie were excited to find not only more spacious rooms, but more playing fields as well. And there was a track for running, too!

At the same time, the School for the Sons of Missionaries changed its name to Eltham College. (In England, some elementary and high schools are called "colleges.")

Eltham now seemed like home to Eric and Rob, having lived there for more than three years. In those three years, while they had not seen anyone in their family, Mary wrote them often from China. When Rob (and sometimes Eric) wrote back, they didn't have to pretend they were happy for their parents' sake—they were!

Dear Mother and Father—and Jenny, too,

So far, so good at the "new" school! Same boys, same teachers (why couldn't that change?), same schoolwork. You will be pleased when you see my marks for this term (Eric will write you later). Eric is doing all right. Did you know he was in a play? Eric played the dormouse in "Alice in Wonderland," and now everyone is calling him "Mouse"!

But the "Mouse" is not quite like his name. After three years of going through this silly game of knotted handkerchiefs (remember?), your son Eric has finally put a stop to it!

Eric felt sorry for this new boy so he said, "That's enough!" And everyone just stopped doing it. Everyone likes Eric, that's for sure, and I think they think he's different from them (could I tell them stories!).

You may not have heard that Headmaster Hayward has retired. (How old was he?) Our new head is named Robertson, and he seems okay except for one of his rules.

This was so funny, and Eric says it's okay to tell you.

It all started when the head said no one could ride his bicycle in the quadrangle.* He said it so

---

*The area between school buildings that is like a courtyard, with grass and sidewalks.

many times, we were tired of hearing it. I mean, who would break this rule?

Well, one afternoon when no one was around, guess who comes riding his bicycle in the quad? None other than Headmaster Robertson himself, with his young son on top of the handlebars! I'm sure he thought no one was watching him.

At that moment your son Eric just happened to be gazing out at nature. When he heard the wheels of the bicycle, he couldn't control himself. So he yells, "Hey, no cycling there!" And then he ducks back inside his room.

I hope you're laughing now! Anyway, the head recognized Eric's voice and sent him to his room without dinner that night, but I don't think he's mad at Eric.

We are going swimming again this afternoon, and I am excited. As you know, we don't have a pool here at the new Eltham, so we must travel by train to the Baths at Ladywell.* The boys are already after Eric to do his funny routine again. After wrapping a wet towel around himself, he pretends like he's receiving the "Order of the Bath" from the King.† We can't stop laughing because he looks so silly.

---

*"Baths" is another name for a pool.

†An award given to worthy gentlemen for great achievement.

Your last letter said we would see you soon. We hope so. Eric sends his love, too.

Your son, Rob

It wasn't long before the family was all together again. When Mary, James, and Jenny arrived in London in 1914—along with a new baby brother, Ernest—they immediately rented an apartment for a year. Rob and Eric were only too happy to move out of Eltham and live with their family, while still going to school during the day.

But the year went by quickly, and all too soon the two teenagers found themselves back at Eltham as roommates once again. Although they were well liked at school, they were still each other's best friend. And they were still each other's main competition in sports.

Both boys earned their "flannels" and "colours" (varsity letters) in rugby and cricket for each of their last three years at Eltham. In rugby and cricket, they played side by side on a team; in track, however, they were each other's opponents.

Rob was a senior in 1918, and he was determined not to let his little brother beat him during his final year at Eltham. Their closest race was the 100-yard dash. Runners must "sprint" this distance (run as fast as possible) to have a chance of winning.

As usual, the brothers shook hands before the race. Eric wanted to win, but at the same time, he wanted Rob to win, too. When the gun sounded, Rob got off to a better start, but

Eric soon caught up with him. The other runners had dropped back. Only the finish line flapped just ahead in the wind.

Throwing his head back and his chest out, Eric crossed the line just ahead of Rob, winning by only a step. He had tied the school record: 10.8 seconds.

Rob, however, was quick to even the score, winning the steeplechase (a combination of hurdles and running), the high jump, and the hurdles. Eric, who later won the 440-yard race and the long jump, was voted Eltham's best overall athlete for 1918.

With Rob at the Medical College of Edinburgh University, Eric became more of a campus leader. At a race in 1919, Eric beat his old record for the 100-yard dash, with a time of 10.2 seconds. That record would not be broken at Eltham for eighty years!

But it was away from the playing fields that Headmaster Robertson said of Eric, "He knew what he stood for." Although not required by the school, Eric began attending Bible studies regularly. He also began visiting the sick at a nearby mission. At school, he was a friend to all boys, but especially those who were not so able as he.

In the spring of 1920, Mary, Jenny, and Ernest came home again. This time, they rented a house in Edinburgh, Scotland, where Rob attended the university. Eric had plans himself to join Rob in the fall. That summer, the Olympic games were once again the talk of the Liddell household.

Mary shook her head as her grown sons read every newspaper article, eager for the race times from Antwerp, Belgium. "Who'll be the next Wyndham Halswelle?" she asked, laughing.

Shrugging his shoulders, Rob pointed to Eric, who seemed to hold the papers higher at the mention of his name.

"Yes, Rob, I think he's sitting right here, too," Jenny chimed in.

Edinburgh, Scotland, 1921–1923

Looking around him, Eric couldn't believe a place like Powderhall Stadium even existed. For one thing, the oval-shaped track was paved with cinders, not grass or dirt. Taking a deep breath, he took in the empty stadium stands, the deep blue sky, the perfectly shaped coal black track, and the yipping sounds of barking dogs! Powderhall was also home to greyhound racing, a popular betting sport in Scotland.

But that wasn't all. Eric almost started laughing as he watched several athletes prepare to begin their training. As soon as they arrived, they took off their long overcoats to reveal (to Eric) silly-looking baggy shorts. Then they began jumping up and down and stretching their arms and legs in all directions.

As he looked down at his feet to keep from laughing, Eric saw the shadow of a man approaching. And then he felt a tap on his shoulder.

"Excuse me, but you are Eric Liddell, are you not?"

Straightening, Eric looked up slightly to face the older man. "I am."

"Tom McKerchar," the smiling man said, extending his hand. "I'm an athletics trainer at the university. I was told I'd find you here."

As he shook his sturdy, well-muscled hand, Eric was at a loss for words. He had come to Powderhall just to check out the place, not to enlist the help of a full-time trainer. Yes, he'd been told he should start "training," but did that mean he had to have someone watching him all the time? "I'm sorry, Mr. McKerchar, but I didn't realize you were told to work with me. I just run, that's all. I mean, what more can you tell me than to run as fast as I can?"

Rubbing his chin, Tom McKerchar looked at the ground and then into Eric's bright blue eyes. "Well, young man, let's just say I've seen you race. . . ."

Just a few months ago, in May of 1921, Eric had entered the University Annual Sports Races, his first competition since his days at Eltham. A friend at the university had heard he could run and had talked him into entering. To the surprise of many, Eric placed second in the first heat of the 100-yard dash—and then went on to win the final in that event with a time of 10.4 seconds. To win, Eric had beaten Innes Stewart, the reigning Scottish champion.

At the same event, Eric entered the 220-yard race and lost by two inches to Stewart. Little did Eric know that, in his entire running career, he would never lose another race in Scotland!

Tom McKerchar had never seen anyone run like Eric Liddell. To Tom, Eric looked more like a prancing circus pony than a world-class runner.

But Tom McKerchar knew he could work with Eric, and he knew he could help Eric run faster even if he didn't change his unusual "windmill" style. First, though, Eric had to want to work with him. Patting him on the back, Tom said, "Eric, you're an unusual young man. Why don't you think about the training and let me know?"

That night Eric asked his mother what she thought. Sitting with him at the kitchen table, she reached for Eric's strong hand. Eric loved the feel of her hands, hands made strong by work and years spent in the harsh Chinese climate. Hands that had always calmed him and then gently urged him in the right direction. Hands that prayed to God.

"Mother, does God really want me to run?"

Turning his hand several times in her own, the older woman then looked at her grown son. "God has given you a tremendous gift, Eric. Of that I am sure."

"But you know my plans. You know that I have always wanted to work with Father in China. How will my running—and now all this training—help me get there?"

"You won't go to China for a few years, Eric. And how long can you run like this? I believe the answer is the same: a few years. Perhaps this is God's plan. To run now, and to give God all the glory for your gift."

Eric's face broke out into a huge grin, and he nodded his head repeatedly. "You know, when I run, I do feel like I'm running for God. Guess tomorrow they can start laughing at me at good old Powderhall!"

In Europe at this time, all athletic training was done only within the confines of a stadium—never in public! It was considered shocking to exercise outside, especially in shorts. So, Eric and Tom met regularly at Powderhall Stadium to train for Eric's upcoming races.

Tom showed Eric how to leave the starting "holes" sooner, how to bring down his knees a bit, and how to cross the finish line most effectively. Most importantly, Tom told Eric not to stop running right after he finished a race but to go a little farther and gradually cool down his body. He instructed him what to eat before a big race (not a big meal!). Lastly, he always gave Eric a massage after his workouts and races. Tom, a trained masseur, would rub the muscles in Eric's back and legs to prevent them from becoming stiff and sore.

Race after race, Eric began to see how the months of training had helped him. He hadn't stopped winning—and now all of Scotland was cheering for him.

In 1922, Eric set a Scottish record in the 220-yard race, winning it in 21.8 seconds. At this particular competition, Eric entered the 440-yard race as well, winning it in 52.4 seconds. Considered a sprinter, Eric had never competed in that event. Little did he realize how important that would be in two short years!

In the fall of 1922, Mary and James Liddell, along with Jenny and Ernest, prepared to return to China, this time to the town of Tientsin where Eric had been born. As Eric helped them pack what they would need for the trip, he felt far from his usual self. He knew in his heart that they would not be together again for a long time.

Jenny sensed this, too, but she wasn't going to let Eric dampen everyone's spirits. Dragging him by the hand to her room, Jenny announced, "I want you to see what I've had to live with the last two years. Just look under my bed!"

Eric began pulling out box after box filled with his trophies. Little did he realize that Jenny, at the direction of their mother, had saved every token of his many victories. There were gold watches, cake stands, clocks, silver knives and forks, and flower vases, too! Eric rolled over on his back and started laughing and laughing.

"I can't believe you've saved all this—and for what?" he exclaimed, almost out of breath.

"No one will ever need a gold watch in this family, that's why," Jenny answered, also laughing. "But from now on, if you win another race, you find a place for all the cake stands!"

In 1922, Rob was still in medical school at Edinburgh University with a year to go before he would graduate. After their parents left, he and Eric became roommates once again, sharing a house with twelve other students. But while Eric concentrated on his running and studies, Rob decided to speak out about his Christian faith.

Traveling with other students, Rob visited many cities in Scotland and talked about Jesus. But something was missing from these student-led "crusades." The students needed to have a speaker whose name was known in Scotland, someone who would attract a bigger audience. Someone that even people who didn't go to church would recognize and want to meet.

David Thomson, who was a member of Rob's group, was the first to mention Eric's name. He knew Eric had never spoken in public like this, but there was always a first time.

Hitching a ride on a gasoline truck to Edinburgh, David found the house where Eric and Rob were staying. Rob had told David that he couldn't ask his own brother, so David went to see Eric.

The minute David saw Eric, his throat went dry. Eric's picture had appeared in all the newspapers, and his name was always linked with the Olympics, to be held in a little more than a year in Paris. Stumbling over his words, David explained that Eric would be the guest speaker for an audience of all men in Armadale, Scotland.

"Do you. . .er, I mean, could you come and just say a few words? About your faith, I mean, and oh, your running, too—"

Eric looked at the floor for a minute then lifted his head and smiled slowly.

"All right. I'll come."

Right before David Thomson had approached him, Eric

had received this note from Jenny in China: "Fear thou not; for I am with thee: be not dismayed; for I am thy God. Isaiah 41:10. Love, Jenny." Jenny's faith had given Eric the courage to say yes.

That night in Armadale—April 6, 1923—Eric found he had a gift from God he never knew he possessed. He wasn't much of a speaker, but still the eighty men there listened to every word. And these were men who weren't used to coming to lectures. Unemployment was high in this working-class town, and many men spent their free time in the local taverns, not in churches.

Speaking slowly and quietly, he made the men feel like he was having a personal conversation with each one of them. "Do you want to know the God I love? He has given me strength when I thought I had nothing left. And He has given me these words when I thought I couldn't speak."

Eric looked around the room from face to face. "Accept God tonight, and tomorrow you will feel a love you have never known before."

The next day every newspaper in Scotland carried a report of Eric's speech in Armadale. And a week later Eric was asked to speak before a crowd of six hundred! From then on, Eric spent almost every weekend speaking about his faith and his weekdays studying and training for upcoming races. He loved sharing how God wanted everyone to come to know Him—and all that each person had to do was ask Him into his or her life and heart.

While Eric had never felt better in his whole life, there were people who questioned his commitment to running. How would he compete now against the world's best runners? Was he too busy running for the Lord?

CHAPTER 4

Great Britain, 1923–1924

Tom McKerchar slammed down the newspaper in disgust. *If I read one more article like that,* he thought to himself, *I may actually speak to the press for a change!* Tom had made it his policy not to give interviews. *But,* Tom thought, *these writers don't know anything about Eric Liddell.*

Up until the summer of 1923, Eric had only raced in Scotland, and as the competition had not always been "world-class," Eric's times were considered just average. Now, as he prepared for his first race in England, there were those who were doubting Scotland should waste the train fare for him to go. How could such a human windmill win an international race?

Tom scanned the Powderhall track for his star runner and smiled at the sight of his high-pumping legs and gently swaying arms. *Eric looks so happy,* Tom thought, *he must be doing what God wants.*

The race on July 6 and 7, the British Amateur Athletic Association Championships, was considered one of the most important races before the Olympics. Held at London's Stamford Bridge Stadium, the race would feature a long-awaited duel: Eric Liddell, still considered the fastest man in

Scotland, against Harold Abrahams, England's best hope at the Paris games.

Harold, a student at Cambridge University, was from a German Jewish family. Living in England, Harold felt he had been treated differently because he was Jewish. If he could be the fastest man in the world, he thought, maybe then he would be treated like everyone else.

Eric, on the other hand, didn't mind if he was treated differently because of his Christian faith. That just gave him one more opportunity to show God's love—to shake every runner's hand and wish him well, to treat every runner the same, and never to use bad language or tell bad jokes. But Eric still wanted to win. If Harold Abrahams wanted to be the best, he would have to beat Eric Liddell.

The stadium at Stamford Bridge was filled to capacity on Friday, July 6, 1923, as the temperature soared to over 90 degrees Fahrenheit. Men were wiping their foreheads with handkerchiefs, while women fanned themselves with paper fans. All eyes were straining to see the runners on the track.

Eric, the shorter of the two at five feet, nine inches, approached Harold first and shook hands with the tall, dark-haired sprinter. Then they resumed their positions for the 220-yard race.

Earlier that morning, Eric had won his first heat of the 220-yard race in 22.4 seconds. The top three runners in each of the two first heats had advanced to the second heat. Eric knew he would have to get a better start this time. Harold

Abrahams was known for his good starts.

As Eric dug his holes in the track, he couldn't help but glance at the other runners. But Harold's eyes were on the track, deep in concentration. Closing his own eyes, Eric prayed silently, thanking God again for giving him this special ability.

One Bible verse always came to him right before a race, one that Eric liked to describe as the "three sevens," or seventh book of the New Testament, seventh chapter, seventh verse: "But every man hath his proper gift of God, one after this manner, and another after that." Smiling, Eric remembered that was exactly what his mother had said!

As the race official came into view, Eric focused all his attention on the track. After carefully placing his toes in the starting holes, he raised his muscular legs and arched his back just the way Tom had taught him. And then he waited for the gun.

At the sound of the starting pistol, Harold Abrahams exploded from the line, leading the pack by two yards. Once again, Eric had gotten off to a poor start, and he could feel all eyes on him. Swinging his arms, Eric willed himself forward, closer and closer to Abrahams.

From his seat in the stadium, Tom watched the race almost holding his breath, while a stream of perspiration trickled down his cheek. Suddenly, the red-faced Scottish man next to him began jumping up and down. "Look at him now! Aye, he culdna win if his heid's na back!"

As if he had heard his countryman's cry, Eric finally threw his head back, his eyes on the cloudless sky above. Gasps could be heard as the two men pushed to the finish line, each one seeming to throw his chest out farther to gain the advantage.

At the tape Eric Liddell had edged out Harold Abrahams with a win of 21.6 seconds, a blistering pace!

On Saturday, the rumor circulating through the stadium was that Eric and Harold would meet again in the finals of the 100-yard race. Both men had won their first heat of the race—Eric in 10.0 seconds and Harold in 10.2—and now the second heats were about to begin. While Eric set a new British national record in the 100, running the distance in an incredible 9.8 seconds, Harold did not place in the top three of his heat and could not go to the finals.

By the end of the day, Eric had won the 220-yard and the 100-yard events and was awarded the Harvey Memorial Cup as the best British athlete of 1923. His final time in the 100-yard race of 9.7 seconds was another new British record, one that would not be broken for thirty-five years! Eric Liddell was now the reigning British champion in two track events, and the press would not let him forget that.

On the train back to Scotland, Tom showed Eric the latest newspaper articles. "In a week I've gone from goat to glory," Eric exclaimed, laughing.

"Or from black sheep to world's fastest human," joked Tom. "They're even calling you the next Wyndham Halswelle!"

"Good old Wyndham," Eric remembered, smiling. "Now that's something my dad would like to see."

Putting the papers aside, Tom stared out the window for awhile. "We won't know for sure about the Olympics until the race at Stoke-on-Trent in a couple weeks." Tom turned to look at Eric and then playfully punched him in the arm. "But it looks like it's you and me, Wyndham, in Paris next summer."

Eric shook his head, laughing. There was so much to think about now besides Paris. He still wanted to travel around Scotland and share his love of Jesus, and then he couldn't forget his studies at Edinburgh University. He had one year to finish his degree and one more year after that to train to become a minister. And then. . .China!

Retrieving his Bible from his satchel, Eric opened God's Word to 2 Corinthians, chapter 10, verse 17: "But he that glorieth, let him glory in the Lord." As the countryside passed in a blur, Eric tried to focus his thoughts. What was God trying to tell him?

Chapter 5

The Olympics

No other sports competition has driven athletes to train harder than the Olympics. Perhaps one reason is that the Olympics have a tradition like no other sports event, with a history that can be traced back to 776 B.C.—more than seven hundred years before the birth of Jesus.

From that date until A.D. 394, the Olympian games were held at Olympia, Greece. Every four years—known as an "olympiad"—the fastest and strongest men in Greece would compete against each other.

Olympia was important because it was considered the "home" of twelve gods, including Zeus, the "greatest" one of all. The Greek people had created these gods to explain events of nature and everyday occurrences and why good and bad things happened to people. To make these gods "happy," on the first day of the ancient Olympian games the people believed they had to offer sacrifices to them!

In ancient times, the Olympics consisted of one day of footraces (running), followed by a few days of wrestling, javelin and discus throwing, and chariot races. On the final day of the games, the fifth, the closing event was a race between men wearing suits of armor.

Whoever won that race was crowned by the high priest of Zeus with a wreath made from olive branches and leaves. After a poem celebrating his victory was read, the winner was carried home to his native village on the shoulders of his friends. For the rest of his life he would be treated like an emperor—everything he wanted would be given to him!

For more than a thousand years, the Olympian games continued like this until, for some unknown reason, the Roman emperor Theodosius did away with the competition.

But in the late 1800s, a period of history when people were again interested in studying about ancient Greece, a Frenchman named Baron Pierre de Coubertin decided to bring back the Olympic Games—as a worldwide sports competition. Since 1896, the Olympics have been held every four years—except during the two world wars—but in different locations. And, since 1912, women have been allowed to compete, as well.

In 1924, the eighth Olympic Games of "modern" times were to be held in Paris, the home of Baron de Coubertin. The baron was so excited to have the games in his city that he created a special motto just for that Olympic year, a motto taken not from Greek but from Latin.

"Citius, Altius, Fortius!" (That is, translated into English, "Faster, Higher, Stronger!")

Athletes from forty-five countries would be in Paris, including four hundred from the United States alone, a record number. Who would be the strongest, who would jump the highest, who would run the fastest?

The 100-meter race was considered the test for the world's fastest human. From the United States, Charley Paddock and Jackson Scholz were considered the favorites; from New Zealand, Art Porritt was considered a possible medalist; and from Great Britain, Harold Abrahams and Eric Liddell alone carried the hopes of their small nation.

But that was before January 1924—before the timetable for the Olympic races had been released by Baron de Coubertin, and before Eric was faced with the decision that would mark him for the rest of his life!

The Path to Paris, 1924

For many days, Tom McKerchar had been checking the mail at the athletic director's office at Edinburgh University. *The schedule for the Olympics should have been sent by now,* he thought anxiously.

He had heard that this summer Baron de Coubertin wanted the Olympics to last only two weeks, and not the entire summer, as in some past competitions. He also knew that no races would be scheduled for Monday, July 14, a national holiday in France called Bastille Day.

A soft knock on his office door caused Tom to sit up in his chair. "Mr. McKerchar," the athletic director's secretary said, interrupting his thoughts, "I believe it's here." In her hand she waved the official-looking envelope.

Ripping the envelope open, Tom scanned page after page of the lengthy schedule. *There it is,* he thought excitedly, *the 100-meter race. And the first heats are on. . .*

The pages slipped through his hands and fell, one by one, gracefully to the floor. Tom buried his head in his hands for a moment, and then stood, making his way for the door. "Miss Evans, I'll be out for awhile. I need to find Eric if I can."

Dashing back inside the office to retrieve the schedule, he then sped out again just as quickly, catching a glimpse of Miss Evans's surprised face. "And don't tell anyone the schedule is in," he advised sternly. "We don't want reporters hounding Eric—at least, not yet!"

Eric was at the home he shared with several other students, trying to get in a few hours of studying before he left again with David Thomson to give another speech. Since Eric had made the British Olympic team, the demand to hear him had only increased. To all of Scotland, he was already a hero, the man with the best chance to bring home a gold medal.

Tom didn't know what to say, but that was never a problem with Eric. With a broad grin on his face, Eric began telling Tom about his travels for the Lord. Tom tried to pay attention, but Eric was soon aware that his mind was elsewhere. "What is it, Tom? If you don't mind, I have to say you don't look well," Eric said with concern in his voice.

Tom cleared his throat. "It's just—Eric—I know what you're going to say—but I wish I could change your mind."

"Out with it! Only God can read minds." Eric motioned Tom on with his hand.

"The Olympic schedules came in the mail today. You know, the baron is trying to fit all the events and heats into just two weeks. So—"

"So—what is it, Tom?"

"The first heats for the 100-meter race are to be held on a Sunday, Eric. July 6, to be exact."

Without a moment's hesitation, Eric said, "I'm not running." His eyes did not blink, he did not wring his hands, and he did not pace the floor of his room.

Sighing, Tom turned away from him and glanced out the window.

"Tom, do you really know why I can't run? God's Fourth Commandment to Moses said to 'remember the sabbath day,* to keep it holy.' If I run in a race that honors me or other men, I am not remembering God's Sabbath. And if I start ignoring one of God's commands, I may as well ignore all of them. But I can't do that because I love God too much."

Tom nodded his head. Eric had never raced on a Sunday, and he wouldn't change his beliefs now, even for the Olympics. "I'll contact the British authorities. That's the next step," Tom said. "But Eric, are you ready for what will happen? I mean, the reporters?"

---

*The day one sets apart to worship God, usually Sunday.

"Jesus never said that to follow Him would be easy," Eric answered simply.

In the weeks that followed, Tom and the British sports authorities tried desperately to change the date of the first heats. The French officials, however, refused to do that. Instead, Eric was entered in the 200- and 400-meter races, events that he had won before but that he clearly did not dominate. Two other relay events—races that involve four runners on a team—were not considered because their heats also fell on a Sunday.

In the weeks that followed, the attacks by the British press were nonstop. "A traitor to Scottish sporting, to all that Wyndham Halswelle stood for!" proclaimed one paper. Another journalist reported that Eric was not running so he could get more publicity. Again and again, newspapers asked, "Why couldn't Eric run on Sunday and dedicate the race to the Lord?"

Everyone, it seemed, was bothered about Eric's decision except Eric. Even a British nobleman was quoted as saying, "To play the game is the only thing in life that matters."

Eric Liddell had decided he would play the game, but on God's terms. All through the winter and spring, Tom and Eric trained harder and harder for the two events he would run. And in the back of his mind, Eric quoted over and over one favorite verse from the Bible: "Whosoever believeth on him [God] shall not be ashamed" (Romans 10:11).

To him, God meant more, much more, than an Olympic gold medal.

CHAPTER 6

Paris, France, July 1924

Saturday, July 5. *Today it all begins,* Eric thought as he gazed at his reflection in the window of a storefront. And he saw not only his reflection, but the images of many members of the British Olympic team, all dressed alike. Eric and the team—decked out in cream-colored shirts and pants, blue blazers, and white straw hats—were awaiting the signal to begin marching down the Champs Elysees, the grand boulevard of Paris, and then on to the Olympic stadium, known in Paris as the Stade Colombes.

Taking his handkerchief from his jacket pocket, he wiped away a stream of perspiration from the side of his face. The temperature in Paris was already in the 90s, with an expected high of 110 degrees!

Eric filed into line next to Douglas Lowe, his roommate in Paris and one of the favorites to win a medal in the 800-meter race. Just ahead of him was Harold Abrahams, voted captain of the British track team. More than many runners, Harold had understood why Eric couldn't run on Sunday. Because he wanted others to respect his Jewish faith, he, in turn, respected Eric for taking such a brave stand.

At the Arc de Triomphe, the parade of athletes paused

while Britain's Prince of Wales (later King Edward VIII) placed a wreath at the Tomb of the Unknown Soldier, a monument dedicated to those who died in World War I.

Eric felt his heart skip a beat at the entrance to the Olympic stadium. More than sixty thousand spectators filled the stands, and the sound of their applause was like the roar of many oceans.

Nation after nation marched under the "Marathon Gate" into the stadium, led by the first team, the athletes from South Africa. Each team was preceded by its nation's flag and sometimes a band from that country.

Just before Eric and the British team entered, the Queen's Cameron Highlanders began to play their bagpipes and beat their drums. Dressed in Scottish kilts and wearing bearskin headdresses, the Highlanders held special meaning for Eric. He knew he had disappointed Scotland by refusing to run in the 100-meter race. But he still had two races to run. . . .

Finally, Baron de Coubertin gave a short speech and military bands played the French national anthem, "La Marseillaise." Cannons were set off as the Olympic flag with its five rings was raised into the breezeless sky. The eighth Olympics had officially begun!

Sunday, July 6. As Eric made his way to the pulpit of the Scots Kirk, the Scottish Presbyterian church in Paris, Harold Abrahams began digging his holes in the cinder track for the first 100-meter heat. And as Eric arrived back at his hotel in the afternoon, an exhausted Harold was receiving his victory massage from his trainer. Harold had made it through two heats and was ready to run the final on Monday. He would be the only runner from Great Britain in the 100-meter race.

Monday, July 7. Eric tried to ignore the stares from the crowd as he found his seat in the Olympic stadium. He did not have a race to run today, a fact the newspapers had all reported at great length. But he did have a race to watch and a runner to cheer—the tall and muscular Harold Abrahams.

Four Americans were also in the 100-meter final, including the favorite, Charley Paddock, and Jackson Scholz, considered almost his equal. Paddock was the current world record holder, clocking the distance earlier this year in 10.4 seconds. He still held the Olympic record, set at Antwerp in 1920, of 10.8 seconds.

Eric squinted his eyes and cupped his hands over his forehead so he could see better. *Harold looks as determined as ever,* he thought. Eric joined in the cheering until the race official held up his gun.

At the sound of the blast, the runners sprang to life, soaring down one length of the track. With Scholz at his heels, Harold fought for the lead, breaking the finish line first. Harold had set a new Olympic record—10.6 seconds—and won the gold medal!

Jumping up and down in the stands, Eric was happier than most of the excited fans there. In his heart, he knew this had been God's plan. He was to give God glory in his way, as a Christian. And Harold was to show his God-given talent in another. (Harold Abrahams was the first British runner to win a gold medal at the Olympics; no European runner would win this event again until the 1980 Olympics.)

Tuesday, July 8. Tom McKerchar and Eric shared a taxi to the Olympic stadium, but their ride was a silent one. *Today is the day,* Tom thought, *for Eric to prove all those reporters wrong, and all those so-called nobles.* His face catching the breeze from the open window, Eric thought, *Today is the day for me just to run my race.*

As they walked around the track, Tom shook his head. "It doesn't look good, Eric. They've just laid new cinders, and the track is not packed very tightly. Times should be slower."

"Not to mention the heat! Now I know why my ancestors settled in Scotland," Eric answered lightly. "And please don't look so serious, Tom. This is why I run—to be in races like this."

Shaking his head, Tom found his seat in the stands as Eric joined the other runners for the first heats of the 200-meter race. Later, both men were proved right. The times for all the top runners were slower, but all the top runners came through. The stage was set for Wednesday's 200-meter semifinal and final races.

Wednesday, July 9. As temperatures again soared into the 100s, Eric again found his place on the track for his semifinal race. In the 200-meter race, runners would make one turn, covering exactly half of the oval track.

Eric knew this race might be as tough as the final, if he made it there. To his left was the great American runner, Charley Paddock. Paddock had finished in fifth place in the 100-meter race, and it was clear he wanted revenge. Harold had run in the first semifinal of the day and barely made it to the finals with a third-place finish. Eric acknowledged his friend on the sidelines with a wave. He knew he couldn't let Harold alone carry the British team into the finals.

At the start of the gun, Paddock leaped ahead of Eric, until Eric put his arms in motion. Then, for a few strides, the men ran side by side. At the finish tape, Paddock edged out Eric, winning the semifinal in 21.8 seconds, just one-tenth of a second faster than the Scottish runner. Eric had made it to the finals—but could he run this hard again?

The finals for the 200 meters were to be held in the late afternoon, but the lane assignments were posted soon after the semifinals. Harold would be in lane two, the second from the most inside lane; Jackson Scholz was in lane four; Eric had been given lane five; and Charley Paddock was in the most outside lane, lane six. All in all, six runners had made it to the finals.

As the race began, Eric doubted he had the energy to finish in the top three. Charley Paddock got off to a fast start, followed closely by Jackson Scholz. Harold was somewhere behind Eric, the heat having sapped his strength, as well.

Remembering Tom's advice, Eric pumped his knees higher and threw out his chest. At the finish line, Eric had edged out two runners to gain third place. He had won the bronze medal!

Eric had become the first Scot in Olympic history to win a medal in the 200 meters, and the first Scot to win any medal since the famed Wyndham Halswelle in 1908. Even the newspapers were kind to him, with one reporter writing, "As usual, Liddell did not start too well, but made a wonderfully fast finish."

After hugging Tom and Harold at the same time, Eric quickly made his way down the stairs to the dressing rooms, located below the stadium. There would be no victory laps, no flag waving, no fist pumping. That was not Eric's style.

But tomorrow he would be back on the cinder track. Back to prove he could still run the 400-meter race, even though he was far from the favorite.

Paris, France, Friday, July 11, 1924

Outside the Hotel Moderne, Eric waited, pacing back and forth. He was to meet Tom and a few other British runners there so they could arrive at the same time at the stadium. After Thursday's heats, he seemed to feel every muscle of his body. He had run more races in a few days than he had in a month!

Then Eric saw a familiar face. Running up to him was the masseur the British team had hired just for the Olympics.

Occasionally, he had helped Tom give Eric a massage. Eric extended his hand and patted the older man on the back. But the masseur said only a few words and handed Eric a small piece of paper that had been folded once. Then he turned just as quickly to go.

"Thanks, I'll read it at the stadium!" Eric called to him, puzzled that the man hadn't wanted to have a conversation. Shrugging his shoulders, Eric put the paper in his pocket. And then it was forgotten as Tom and the others greeted him.

After the semifinal heats had been run that afternoon, six runners had qualified for the final 400-meter race, to be held at 6:30 that evening. The favorites were two Americans, Horatio Fitch and J. C. Taylor; Joseph Imbach of Switzerland and D. M. Johnson of Canada were also contenders. Guy Butler, Britain's silver medalist at Antwerp in this event, was still in the race but he had injured his leg. With his thigh heavily bandaged, he would not be able to crouch down into the traditional starting position.

And then there was Eric. He had been given lane six for a starting position, the dreaded outside position.

As he plopped down in a chair in the dressing room, Eric had never felt so tired. *In just two hours I'll have to run the race of my life,* he thought desperately.

Reaching inside his coat pocket, he happened upon the paper given to him hours before. Unfolding the now-crumpled square, Eric quickly read the message. Then, bowing his head, Eric whispered, "Thank You, God."

Written with care, the message read, "In the old book it says, 'Them that honour me I will honour.' Wishing you the best of success always." The "old book" was the Bible; the quotation was from 1 Samuel 2:30, a verse Eric himself had always loved. Yes, he had always tried to honor God, even though he was far from perfect. And while others might think that he expected God to help him win the 400-meter race this evening, Eric knew God had blessed him in countless ways already.

As race time approached, Eric laced on his leather running shoes and walked slowly up the stairs to the familiar cinder track. Deafening cheers arose from the crowd at the sight of the runners, especially the Americans Fitch and Taylor. The stars and stripes of the American flag were waving everywhere Eric looked.

Nudging Guy Butler with his elbow, Eric joked, "Has someone forgotten to tell them that two Brits are still in the race?"

Guy tried to smile. "Look at me, Eric. They know I'll never win with this leg, even if I give it all I have. Besides, this is Fitch's event—he'll be trying to beat his own Olympic record." Just that afternoon Fitch had won his semifinal heat with a time of 47.8 seconds.

The time for the runners' warm-ups around the track was ending as the race official in his long white coat approached the cinder oval. But just at that moment, the blaring of horns and the pounding of drums could be heard from outside the Marathon Gate, the formal entrance to the stadium.

The Queen's Cameron Highlanders had arrived—and no official could stop them from marching around the track! Dressed in their full costume—Scottish kilts and bearskin headdresses—they proceeded to play the traditional Scottish "fight" song, "The Campbells Are Coming."

Eric and Guy couldn't believe their ears or their eyes. All around them, Union Jacks began flying, the symbol of their country. Now the British fans were on their feet cheering, even as the last wail of a bagpipe faded into the evening air.

In the minutes that followed, Eric once again went from man to man, extending his hand and wishing them well. The Cameron Highlanders had postponed his ritual, one that he had never forgotten. After all these races, the runners had even come to expect this from Eric. To their amazement, he seemed to mean what he said, too.

Clearing his throat, the race official then extended his arm, the pistol pointed to the sky. All the runners were in their starting positions, all except Guy Butler who was almost standing. Eric looked ahead of him, to the first curve of the track. He knew what he had to do.

There was only one way he would win this race. And only God could help him succeed.

In the stands Tom McKerchar held his stopwatch firmly in his hand. As the gun went off, Tom set the timepiece in motion, his eyes fastened on the track. And then his jaw dropped.

Eric was sprinting to the first turn, leading all the runners by more than three meters! Tom blinked his eyes and looked back quickly. And not only that, Guy Butler, bad leg and all, was in second place, his face wrinkled with pain.

Checking his stopwatch halfway through the one-lap race, Tom clocked Eric at 22.2 seconds. At that pace Eric would have won most 200-meter races. No 400-meter runner in his right mind would run that fast—and still have enough left to finish strong. And then Tom saw what he knew would happen: Horatio Fitch had just passed Guy Butler, and his pumping fists were propelling him toward Eric!

Farther back in the pack, Taylor and Imbach, eager to change lanes, had both stumbled briefly. They were now well behind Johnson, Butler, Fitch, and Eric, who was still hanging on to a slim lead.

Now in the final stretch, Tom began pumping his own fists, imitating Eric. There he was, his face to the sky, arms flailing like twin windmills, knees pumping almost to his chest, with the finish tape in sight. Sensing Fitch near him, Eric doubled his efforts, widening the gap between them.

Eric Liddell of Scotland was the first to break the finish tape of the 400-meter race at the 1924 Olympic Games, running at the world-record pace of 47.6 seconds! He was five meters ahead of Horatio Fitch. Guy Butler had bravely finished third.

Clutching his sides, Eric slowed to a stop. He had nothing left to give. After a few minutes, he slowly turned around and walked up to Horatio Fitch and extended his hand and then to Guy Butler, who had collapsed on the grass.

As the band began playing "God Save the Queen," the national anthem of Great Britain, Tom raced toward Eric, his arms extended. "You couldn't just win, you had to go and set a world record!" Tom cried out above the crowd's cheers.

Turning to the crowd, Eric waved briefly. At the end of the race, he had not seen the finish tape—but he had seen hundreds of Union Jacks waving wildly. And now he had brought home the gold medal, the first ever won by a Scotsman. He was not proud of himself, but he was proud of his country.

The following day, Eric was in his hotel room working on another speech he was to give Sunday at the Scots Kirk. He had left the stadium as quietly as he could shortly after the race so he could begin writing. There was no medal ceremony—in 1924 medals were mailed to the athletes several weeks after the games—and he didn't want to talk to too many reporters.

But now a knock on the door made him put down his pen. "Tom, I had a feeling you might drop by," he said to his long-time friend and trainer.

Tom was holding an armful of newspapers, his smile lighting up his face. "In case you have any doubts, you're an official Scottish hero!"

Teasing him, Eric began to push Tom out the door. "I don't want to know any more, Tom. Wasn't it bad enough when I was the next Wyndham Halswelle?"

"Aye, that it was. But now you're the next Rob Roy and William Wallace* rolled into one! Listen to this," he continued, reading from the London paper. " 'No longer a traitor to his country, Eric Liddell is the greatest quarter miler ever!' And there's even a quote from the Flying Scotsman himself."

Eric groaned loudly. He had hesitated saying anything to the press for fear his words would sound too proud. But he did want to share his faith in some way. That was why he came to Paris in the first place.

" 'The secret of my success over the 400 meters,' Mr. Liddell explained, 'is that I run the first 200 meters as hard as I can. Then, for the second 200 meters, with God's help, I run harder.' Spoken like a real hero, if I may say so myself," Tom added.

A few days later, after crossing the English Channel from France to England, the British Olympic team boarded a train for London's Victoria Station. Crowds surrounded Eric as he descended the platform and then joined the parade as he was carried on the shoulders of his fellow Scotsmen to his next train—the one that would take him home to Edinburgh.

At the 1924 Olympics Eric Liddell had indeed been *"Citius, Altius, Fortius"*—but he had also been much more. Now God was calling him to a greater race, one in which there would be no medals and no applause.

---

*Two Scottish heroes.

CHAPTER 7

Tientsin, China, 1925–1935

At last Eric was alone. He had said good-bye to his "family" in Scotland, those thousands of countrymen and women who had followed his running career, and he would soon say hello to his own family in China. As the Trans-Siberian Railway rattled across the barren steppes of Siberia, on its way from Chelyabinsk to Vladivostok, Eric closed his eyes and lay back against the cushioned seat.

For a year, he had been treated like the Olympic champions of ancient times. First, at his graduation from Edinburgh University, he was crowned with a wreath (not of olive branches but oleaster, native to Scotland) and read a poem written just for him. Then he was carried on the shoulders of his fellow students all around town!

When the day came for him to leave his beloved Edinburgh, again hundreds met him at his home to carry the Olympic champion in a beribboned carriage to the train station. As the train was slowly leaving Waverley Station, he leaned out the window, trying to think of something to say. Mobbed by his adoring Scots, Eric decided to sing the hymn "Jesus Shall Reign Where'er the Sun"—and soon everyone was singing with him!

He suddenly laughed out loud, and then quickly brought his hand over his mouth. Most of his fellow Asian passengers wouldn't understand who he was or what had happened to him. Rolling up his sleeves, he decided to read a report on China sent to him by his father. *It's time to dig my holes for a new race,* Eric thought to himself. *The last time I was in China, I was six years old.*

While the Boxers with their karate-style chops were no more, the Chinese people had a new reason to feel afraid. Although a very small nation, Japan was becoming a world power and was beginning to express interest in perhaps conquering its vast neighbor. In Manchuria to the north, the Chinese warlords with their regional armies were beginning to fight Japanese troops. Soon the entire country might be at war with Japan.

Eric's long journey came to an end in Tientsin, China, and what a journey it had been! From England he had taken a steamer ship across the English Channel and then boarded a train from France to Russia. On the Trans-Siberian Railway, the world's longest train system, he had traversed the width of Siberia and then boarded yet another train that had taken him to northeastern China. James and Mary, and of course Jenny and Ernest, were also in Tientsin, and Rob, now a medical doctor, was in Siaochang at the mission hospital.

Eric had been born in Tientsin, but he had no memories of the dirty, sprawling city. From the city's Devil's Market, thieves, opium dealers, and forgers traded illegal goods. And from grimy narrow alleyways lined with fragile shacks, the city's poor traded almost anything for food.

At the Anglo-Chinese College, however, where he had received an appointment to teach, Eric would have little to do with such desperate people. He would be teaching science, religion, and sports to the sons of Tientsin's middle class and wealthy families. The school's administrators, who were missionaries, believed that by providing a Christian education for the sons of the most successful, the future of China would be better.

And for a time while Eric was there—before war became a fact of life—that was a distinct possibility.

After the first week of classes, Eric collapsed on a chair in the living room of the house he shared with his parents. His mother was preparing dinner, and his father was working on a sermon he would give the following Sunday.

"Eric, you shouldn't be so hard on yourself. You've only been back in China a few months," James Liddell advised him.

"You don't know the latest news, Father. Now the school wants me to teach English, my worst subject. Besides, I've forgotten so much Chinese I can barely talk to my students anyway! How can I tell them about Jesus?" Eric sighed loudly.

"The language you learned as a boy will return to you, but you must study every chance you get, Son. And as for telling the boys about Jesus. . ."

Eric peered closely at the white-haired minister and missionary. "Yes, Father?"

"Remember your God-given talents, your running, your love of sports. They know nothing about you now—"

Smiling again, Eric slapped his leg excitedly. "I see what you mean! But Father, that means—well, you know what they wear!"

All boys at the Anglo-Chinese College wore the school uniform—a floor-length, long-sleeved, dark blue cotton robe—for all school activities, including sports. That made learning any sport, especially those that involved running and kicking a ball, very difficult. After weeks of wondering what he should do, finally Eric took a drastic step. One day he stood before his students—in a tank top and shorts!

Running up and down the school's tiny grassy field, Eric showed them how easy and fun sports could be. At first the boys laughed, and then they started rolling up their robes. Desperate, Eric pleaded with the school directors to let the boys wear shorts only for learning sports. When the decision was made, Eric became a very popular teacher.

As the boys' skills increased, Eric noticed another obvious need. The school had no real playing fields for games, and in fact, in the entire city of Tientsin, the second-largest city in China, no stadium existed for athletic competition. A few years later, the Min Yuan Sports Field was completed under Eric's supervision. It was a sports arena modeled after London's Stamford Bridge Stadium where Eric had run some of his greatest races.

His students were drawn to him because of his sports skills—and Eric used that love to tell them about his best friend, Jesus Christ. As the months and years passed, even the most difficult boys decided to follow Jesus and to be baptized.

In the fall of 1929, because of failing health, James and Mary Liddell decided to leave the mission field and go home to Scotland. They did not want to go, not when their entire family was at last together in the same country, but they had no choice. Eric had said good-bye to them many times over the years but had never felt so alone.

As he faced his mother at the gangplank to the steamer ship, his voice cracked and he quickly wiped away a tear from his cheek. Mary's face was wet with tears, too. "I will miss you more than I can say," he whispered. His voice stopped as he buried his head in her shoulder.

"Eric, look at me. Perhaps now you can meet someone. . . ."

"She would have to be just like you, you know," he said, winking at her, his sense of humor surfacing again. "So don't hold your breath!"

Eric could joke with his mother, but in the months that followed, he missed their home life, even though he was enjoying his new apartment near the school. On Sundays, he attended his father's church where he had recently been appointed superintendent of the Sunday school. Before Sunday classes began, the children would gather for singing, led by Eric himself.

Eric arrived at church earlier than usual on this winter morning in late 1929. He wanted to meet with the new organist to go over some songs he wanted to teach the children. Hearing a door close at the end of the sanctuary, Eric turned around. A slender young woman, her short black curls bobbing up and down, was walking rapidly toward him.

"Hello, Eric," she said softly. "You don't remember me, do you?"

Eric couldn't help but smile at her shining face and mischievous dark flashing eyes. There was something familiar about her. "Has it been a few years?" he guessed.

"Oh, very good, yes, it has. And I was a young girl then, so you probably did not notice me."

Eric laughed and rubbed his chin. "I can't imagine how I'd forget a face like yours. But I'd like to know where we met, Miss, er—"

"Florence McKenzie. And it was Pei-tai-ho, the summer of 1925, right after you arrived from Scotland. I was only fourteen, but you still played games with me and my sister, and, of course, all the other children there. We've just returned to Tientsin for another mission assignment, so here I am."

"Well, Miss McKenzie, shall we begin?" Nervously Eric pointed to the music, not sure what to say.

Florence's parents, who were missionaries from Canada, had moved into a house not far from the Liddells' former home. And like Eric's parents, they enjoyed a house full of life, with people coming in and out, a house filled with laughter and singing. Eric felt immediately at home there, even though his thoughts about Florence were far from comforting. Only God knew that Eric had fallen in love.

Florence had loved Eric from the time she first met him, but she also had told no one. Her heart beat faster when she caught Eric staring at her, or when he touched her arm to get her attention.

During the summer of 1930, the McKenzies and Eric, along with many other missionary families, vacationed again at Pei-tai-ho. As soon as he returned, Eric sent a telegram to Mary and Jenny—with a very particular request.

A few months later, the package Eric had been waiting for arrived. The McKenzies were due to return to Canada in the next few weeks, and Florence had been accepted at nursing school in Toronto. Eric's furlough was also coming up, when he would return to Scotland. There was no time to waste!

As they were walking to Florence's home after church in late fall, Eric reached gently for Florence's hand. "Flossie, I've got something to say, something I've wanted to say for such a long time."

Eric always called her Flossie when he was teasing her, so Florence wrinkled up her nose. "Oh no, what is it now, Eric? Am I hitting wrong notes every Sunday?"

Laughing, he stopped and gathered both her hands into his and then kissed her.

"No, no, nothing like that. Anyway, I'm trying to be serious. Will you marry me?" he whispered.

Florence threw her arms around his neck and held him close. "I thought you'd never ask!" As she opened the package, lovingly wrapped by Mary and Jenny, she cried in delight at the lovely five-stone diamond engagement ring.

"This is just like the ring my father gave my mother," Eric said. "Because you are the only woman I want to share my life with," he added.

Four years later, on March 27, 1934, Eric and Florence were married in Tientsin, and one year later they welcomed their first child. As he gazed into the face of his newborn daughter, Patricia, Eric smiled at his wife and felt his own eyes fill with tears.

Only God knows the future, but I'm determined that we'll never be apart—unlike my family, Eric thought. *But,* he added suddenly, *only God knows the future.*

From Siaochang to Weihsien, 1937–1945

The old rusted truck managed to sink its tires in every pothole along the dusty country road. Bouncing up and down in the passenger seat, Eric felt his legs and arms ache. He longed to get out and stretch his body. He longed to be back in Tientsin.

More than two years ago, the London Mission Society had asked if he would consider carrying on his mission work at Siaochang, the home of his boyhood. Many missionaries had left and the need was great.

But there were so many reasons not to go. Because of the nearing Japanese armies, China's Great Plain had become a dangerous place. Florence and his two daughters—baby Heather was one year old—would not be safe there. Then there was the drought. People were starving to death because nothing would grow on their farms—and people were killing each other just for food.

As the mud gates of Siaochang came into view, Eric thought about himself. *I'm not a village pastor, I'm a teacher. Just because I lived here doesn't mean I'll know how to help these people. Why, God, why am I here?*

Before he had left Tientsin, Florence had answered that

question for him. She had never known Eric as the Olympic champion, but she did know her husband. "Eric, you knew it was wrong to run on Sunday, and you know it's wrong not to go where God has called you. You have no choice but to go."

Even though almost thirty years had passed, the people of Siaochang still remembered Eric, and they remembered the wonderful work of his parents. "Thank you for coming, *Li-Mu-Shi!*" they cried as they circled him. *Li-Mu-Shi* was the name they had given James Liddell, a name that means "Pastor."

"I'm glad you're here, too," a familiar voice exclaimed behind him.

Turning, Eric gave his brother Rob a big hug. He had left his family, but he was not alone. To his surprise, his feelings of despair had vanished, and his heart was filled with joy. Yes, he was needed here.

Tens of thousands of people lived in the tiny villages on the Great Plain, villages that had been terrorized by bandits, Japanese soldiers, and the drought. So, week after week, Eric and his interpreter Wang Feng Chou—Eric couldn't understand the rural Chinese dialects—visited different places on bicycle.

Before he and Wang entered a village, they would be asked to recognize one or two Chinese characters written on a blackboard. Only those who lived on the Plain would know what they meant.

Eric had little to give the villagers except a message of

hope, a message from God's Word. Sometimes the villages had almost been burned to the ground; other times soldiers were already stationed there. In every town, all men under the age of forty-five had been sent to fight in the Chinese army.

Once, as Eric was holding a church service, the sounds of gunfire echoed close by outside. Instead of giving in to his fear, Eric started singing and soon those present joined in, too. At the end of their service, the people raced outside to their homes, suspecting the worst. But the Japanese soldiers had been shooting at bandits and were not interested in robbing the people or harming their village.

As 1938 came to an end and Rob was due to take his furlough, Eric learned first aid and took on medical duties, as well. The mission had come to be known as a rescue station, and Eric wouldn't turn away anyone, Japanese or Chinese.

It was because of this attitude that the Siaochang mission was in danger of closing. By 1939, the Japanese flag hung over the entrance to the mission, in an effort to scare people away. Clearly the Japanese wanted missionaries like Eric out of Siaochang because they prevented them from assuming complete control of the area. By February 1940, the mission had closed forever.

Eric returned to Tientsin, glad to be together with his family, but sad about the situation in Siaochang. He knew, however, that he and Florence would not be together long. The war was spreading, and China was no place for them to be. Booking passage for his family on a ship bound for

Canada, he said good-bye to Florence and his two daughters. He hoped he would join them soon, but he still felt his place as a missionary was in China.

Kissing Florence's dark curls, Eric said softly, "Those who love God never meet for the last time." His mother had said that to him once when she left him at Eltham, and he had never forgotten it.

In the months that followed, Great Britain and the United States entered into what came to be known as World War II. Japan, faced with the problem of hundreds of Westerners still living in China, decided to create "internment camps" for them. Westerners were Americans and Europeans—some missionaries and businesspeople—who had not found a way out of China.

But to the Japanese, these Westerners were "British and American enemies"—and they would be treated as such. Eric Liddell was now a prisoner of the Japanese, but he was still God's missionary.

On March 30, 1943, Eric arrived at the Weihsien internment camp, hundreds of miles west of Tientsin. He had been allowed to bring only three suitcases. High walls and electric fences surrounded the camp, and powerful searchlights circled the area continually all through the night. Eric was one of eighteen hundred prisoners, more than half of whom were children.

All prisoners were assigned jobs to do, and Eric took on more than anyone. Known as "Uncle Eric," he was the children's math teacher, coach and teacher of all sports, minister of chapel services, supervisor of a dormitory—and friend to all.

But as the months passed, he was working too hard and not taking care of himself. Supplies were few and many people at the camp began starving to death. Eric, always muscular and fit, now looked shrunken and painfully thin.

Even though there was no equipment in the hospital to make an accurate diagnosis, the doctors and nurses at the camp knew Eric was dying. And Eric knew it, too. Still, he never stopped smiling, he never gave up hope, and he never lost his faith in God.

Shortly before he died on February 21, 1945, Eric scribbled a message to a missionary nurse. On a small scrap of paper he had written the first line of his favorite hymn, "Be still my soul." The Olympic champion whose windmill style was a study in motion, and whose love of God was known around the world, was finally at rest.

"I have fought a good fight, I have finished my course, I have kept the faith."

So wrote Paul to Timothy. So lived Eric Liddell.

BILLY GRAHAM

THE GREAT EVANGELIST

by Sam Wellman

Chapter 1

Every morning long before the sun came up, Billy trudged to the barn with his father to milk cows. It was 1924, and Billy was nearly six years old. He could already milk a cow almost as fast as a man could. It was a good thing, too, because his father, Frank, owned over twenty milk cows. Folks around Charlotte, North Carolina, bought a lot of milk from his father's dairy.

"Seems mighty peculiar the way cows fill up with milk again so fast, Daddy," said Billy in the darkness of the barn, thinking about milking the cows again that afternoon.

"It's the Lord's blessing," said his father.

"Sure enough is, Sir," agreed Billy quickly. He quit talking.

Billy knew when to be quiet—most of the time. His daddy could yank him off his milking stool and whop him on the bottom before Billy knew what had happened. It seemed his daddy had six hands to get all that done so fast. His daddy didn't get mad or anything. He just grabbed Billy like he grabbed a squawking hen for Sunday dinner and did what he had to do. And his daddy never blinked an eye.

"It's real pleasant in the barn, Daddy," volunteered Billy. The air was sweet with the smell of hay and milk and cows. He got along fine with the cows. He liked them. And they liked him. One cow stepped on his foot once. But that was a pure accident.

After milking, Billy got to go outside and feed the chickens and the goats. He liked chickens. But, oh, those wonderful goats! He liked them so much. And they liked him. Goats were just about the warmest, smartest, funniest critters on earth. And they were so friendly.

After Billy finished his chores, he washed up and sat down to eat a breakfast of grapefruit, eggs, sausage, grits, toast, and chocolate milk. He heard his mother say, "Maybe today will be the day when the Lord comes again." She said that every morning. There was deep longing in her voice.

"Yes, Ma'am," mumbled Billy as he wiped milk off his mouth.

His mother asked, "Do you remember Proverbs 3:5–6 that I taught you?"

"Trust in the LORD with all thine heart; and lean not unto thine own understanding. In all thy ways acknowledge him, and he shall direct thy paths."

"That's just fine, Billy," said his mother.

"Isn't this the time of year we pull up the sweet potatoes, Daddy?" asked Billy.

"It's September and that's the right time of the year to pull sweet potatoes, but you're going to be in school," answered his father.

"School! When?" blurted Billy.

"Today," said his mother. She looked worried.

"Today?" cried Billy.

"Go get your good clothes on," said his father. "You've

seen the school bus go by our farm a hundred times. You even wave at the bus driver. Well, today you get to ride that bus."

Billy liked the bus driver. He liked just about everybody. In fact, now that he thought about it, he did like everybody. And it was a fact that just about everybody liked Billy. Was there anybody who didn't just about melt when Billy grinned ear to ear? Billy dressed quickly and sat in the living room, fretting over school. He had never been to school before. He could hear his parents talking in the kitchen. Their voices were warm and friendly.

"Billy's going to be tall and lean like you, Frank," said his mother.

"But he's got your blond hair, Morrow," said Billy's father. "And by dogs if he doesn't have his granddaddy Crook Graham's eyes! Those blue eyes could stare right through a plate of lead."

"Granddaddy Crook Graham was mighty ornery." His mother's voice was worried now. "How do you think Billy will do in school?"

"He doesn't seem to ever get tired." His father's deep voice was weary. "Has that boy been eating sweets?"

"Nothing more than an apple or a pear," said Billy's mother quickly.

Billy's skin crawled as he listened. Suzie, the cook, kept a jar of candies on the back porch. So Billy and his younger sister, Catherine, ate a lot of sweets. *Oh God, please don't let Suzie get in trouble,* Billy prayed. Billy liked Suzie so much. And she liked Billy.

"Billy will start school in a few minutes, and everybody in Mecklenburg County will know about him then," groaned his father.

"We won't let the devil win," said his mother. "We'll pray and pray and pray."

"But Billy pushed a dresser out of an upstairs bedroom into the hall and plumb down the stairs," said his father. "You saw him at the top of the stairs. He just grinned at you like a puppy dog. And out in the hen house he overturned a basket of eggs."

"He knocks dishes off the center of the table," sighed his mother.

"I didn't know that!" snapped Billy's father. "He's going to get a good whipping for that."

Billy fumed as he listened. Didn't his mother already whip him for that? She got out that switch of hers and really whopped him. He was sure of it. But he was too smart to complain. That only made Daddy lay it on heavier. Billy would just grin. That worked about as well as anything.

"Let us pray Billy is going to outgrow this rebellion," added Billy's mother. "Oh, how we must pray."

The Grahams prayed a lot. Billy's mother had said from memory many times, " 'Love the LORD thy God with all thine heart, and with all thy soul, and with all thy might. And these words, which I command thee this day, shall be in thine heart: And thou shalt teach them diligently unto thy children, and shalt talk of them when thou sittest in thine house.' "

Billy peeked into the kitchen. Tears ran down his father's cheeks. Arms raised toward the ceiling, his father prayed in a trembling voice, "Oh, Lord, help a wayward child."

How his father could pray!

That night when Billy returned on the school bus to the Graham farmhouse, his mother rushed out of the house. "How was your first day of school, Billy?" she asked anxiously.

"I don't think the teacher likes me," answered Billy.

"Oh no! What did you do, Billy?" His mother's eyes looked around the farm as if searching for Billy's father.

"I didn't do anything." And he wasn't going to do anything at school, either. Not after his daddy talked to him before Billy left that morning on the bus. If Billy ever wanted to play with his gang of goats or play baseball or play Tarzan or ever do anything fun again, he'd better not get in trouble at school. And his daddy's eyes hadn't blinked once.

"But why doesn't the teacher like you?" asked his mother, interrupting Billy's thoughts.

"I don't know." The truth was Billy had been so afraid of getting in trouble he forgot to smile. He was dressed as smart as if he was going to Sunday school, but he forgot to smile. And the teacher didn't even know he was alive.

"You take her a little bouquet of flowers tomorrow," suggested his mother.

"I don't know how." And Billy went inside to change into his work clothes. On his way to the barn, a flock of bleats and purrs and whimpers collected behind him. *Say, that would make a great trick,* thought Billy. He would teach his flock of goats and dogs and cats to trail behind him as he rode his bike. He would practice and practice. He had to use his time better at home. Because grade school sure wasn't going to be any fun.

The next morning after chores and breakfast, Billy rushed outside to ride his bike. Before the school bus appeared, he had his flock trailing behind him. He rode up and down the gravel road in front of the house. Several cars honked at him in delight. He grinned and waved. What a great trick!

But there came the bus. He waved to the driver, then rode back and forth awhile. Finally the bus driver wasn't laughing anymore. Billy dumped his bike.

As he got on the bus, Billy's mother handed him a small bouquet of flowers. "Now you give these to your teacher," she said.

Billy got off the bus at the one-story brick school building surrounded by a wasteland of dirt packed down by flying feet. He walked right past frowning kids into the school and handed the bouquet to the teacher. This time he didn't forget to grin.

"For me?" She saw him for the first time. "What a sunshiny smile! What's your name, Boy?"

"Billy Graham, Ma'am."

CHAPTER 2

Every day from then on was just bursting with school and work and fun. Billy never got tired. Yet when he went to bed, he was asleep so fast he couldn't remember trying to fall asleep.

On Saturdays, Daddy might drive him and Catherine the eight miles over to the farm of Grandma Coffey. There they played in her orchard under long rows of sagging plum and pear and apple trees.

Then Grandma Coffey sat them down to milk and cookies. She told them about Granddaddy Ben Coffey who fought at Gettysburg during the Civil War way back in 1863 and lost his eye and his leg. Then he came back to marry Lucindy Robinson.

"Who?" gasped Billy.

"Me!" his grandmother laughed.

Sometimes Grandma Coffey would tell Billy and Catherine about the days when Billy was born. "One fall day in 1918 your mother had picked butterbeans, then started having a baby that night. It was not until late afternoon the next day, November 7, that you were born, Billy, kicking your legs like a wild frog."

"Did they have to tie a rope to my legs and yank me out?"

"No. Folks don't pull stubborn babies out like they pull out stubborn calves."

Billy was like a different boy in school. His parents couldn't believe it, given the wild way he acted at home, but he was. He hardly said a word in class.

But one second off the school bus in the afternoon and Billy felt so good he would run around behind the bus and turn off its gas valve. Pretty soon the bus would sputter to a stop, and the driver would hop out to stare Billy down. Billy would just grin, and no matter how hard the driver tried to be mad, he couldn't keep from grinning himself.

"It's such great fun being back on the farm again," said Billy. "Even if I do have to do chores and play with Melvin." For Billy now had a baby brother, Melvin, nearly six years younger.

When Billy reached the age of ten, he got to hang around his daddy and Uncle Simon. The two men talked about the gospel—the good news about Jesus—that was told in the Bible.

That was when Billy really learned how hard his daddy worried about his soul. Had his daddy used his life as God wanted? And was he really saved?

His daddy fretting like that began to worry Billy a little. Billy just figured folks went to church and once in awhile tried to remember God's words in the Bible so they knew how to behave, and that was that. A person could pretty much plan on a one-way trip to heaven and eternal glory, whatever that was. But all this worrying by Daddy worried Billy.

And the Scripture from Ecclesiastes that Mother made Billy memorize began to make sense: "Remember now thy

Creator in the days of thy youth, while the evil days come not."

"Sooner or later the Scripture is always proved right," she said, "because it is truly the Word of God."

Billy's daddy built a new two-story brick home with white pillars, landscaped in front with oaks and cedars. It even had water and electricity and inside toilets. Billy's corner bedroom faced a wall of trees behind the house. The room was perfect, except for Melvin snoring in one of the two iron-framed beds.

The dairy was doing very well with its red barns trimmed in white. The farm now had fifty dairy cows, more every day it seemed.

Billy loved baseball like no other game. He loved to pound his fist into the stiffness of a brand new glove. He loved to swing the bat, to hear the loud *whack,* to see the flight of the ball. Those moments were all sweeter than chocolate cake. Once in awhile his bat launched that rare comet that soared so high and so far that playing major league baseball seemed possible some day.

One day Billy couldn't believe his ears when he heard who was coming to Charlotte. "Babe Ruth?" he gasped. "The player who hit sixty home runs in just one season?"

"Yes," Daddy explained, "the Babe is barnstorming between seasons."

And the day came that Billy saw Babe Ruth swing a monstrous bat and blur a baseball into the heavens over Charlotte. If that wasn't enough, Daddy took him up to shake the hand of the moon-faced giant.

"Hi ya, kid," rumbled the Babe as he roughed up Billy's hair.

Also at the age of ten, Billy went on a reading binge. He nibbled his fingernails to the quick as he read books about Tarzan. Acting out the books was fun, too. Deep in a thicket, Billy climbed high on the branches of trees to perch above. What fun it was to observe his bewildered "chimp" Melvin looking for him.

Billy's mother was bewildered, too. "How can you read books all the time, Billy, but not get good grades in school?"

"School doesn't give a test on Tarzan," joked sister Catherine.

Billy managed to get Bs and Cs and Ds. His father just grunted at his report card unless it showed a poor grade in behavior. Then the belt came out. But Billy's mother was upset by Cs and Ds. Billy soothed her by picking bouquets for her every Sunday.

Billy and his mother were very close. Even after he went to high school, he would tell Mother about the girls he thought he liked. And he discussed himself, too. He had been studying the mirror for some time. If being the tallest, thinnest kid in his class wasn't bad enough, his eyes were sinking right back into his head—deeper every year. Lately they had darkened around the edges, so they seemed to be peering out of a cave.

"And my nose and chin jut out fantastically like they do

in those Mother Goose characters," Billy fretted.

Mother reassured him. "Are you worried? A boy with your wavy blond hair and your strong features and your heavenly smile?"

Billy always could fall back on his smile. It did seem like kids warmed up to his smile. So why worry? The girls seemed to like him. He was more relaxed in school now. Once in awhile he spoke up in class. It wasn't so much fear that kept him from talking, as it was he had nothing to say.

Now if they had a course on baseball, he would be a regular chatterbox. He was sure of it, although when he had to give an oral report in English class on a book about baseball, he slouched and mumbled and fumbled for words. His dangly hands groped for a place to hide.

But the older Billy got, the more sure of himself he became. He began to act at school like he acted at home. Love just bubbled out of him. The girls really did like him. And he liked them.

He could have pulled away from his family at this time, feeling more and more comfortable at school. But his family didn't let him. Just because he wore white shirts and bright painted ties and ice-cream slacks and a winning smile to school didn't mean he got out of chores or meals or prayers after supper at home.

The Grahams stayed close, and Billy played with his sister Jean—even though he was fourteen years older. It was a good thing he was anchored in his family because about this time a lot of things happened in his life. With the good came the bad.

One day, Billy knew something bad had happened. Billy's father never said more than a few words, except when he prayed after supper, but he was grumpier than usual. So Billy asked his mother, "What happened?"

"We lost all our money at the bank. Everybody did. Folks are calling this the 'Great Depression.' Some kids may have to drop out of school to go to work. But not you, Billy. We have four hundred regular customers. Folks with kids won't give up their milk, and most of them will keep paying us. And besides, what did the Lord tell us in Luke 12?"

"Take head, and beware of covetousness: for a man's life consisteth not in the abundance of the things which he posesseth."

"Perfect," she said, pleased.

Then his father had an accident. A hired hand had been sawing a plank of wood with a circular saw, and a knot flew off like a cannon ball, striking Frank in the face. From the nose down his face was smashed in. All his front teeth were gone, and that was not the worst of his injuries. At the hospital, he lapsed into a fight with death.

Billy's mother comforted the children, "Don't you remember your father saying the Lord 'is my refuge and my fortress: my God; in him will I trust' from Psalm 91?"

A few years before, Billy had been right there when

Grandma Coffey, about eighty, rose up from her sick bed to cry out that she saw glory's blinding light and the outstretched arms of Jesus. She even saw angels and her dear departed Ben. Then she fell back on the pillow and died!

"She saw the Lord Jesus and heaven," someone said in awe.

Billy knew Jesus and heaven were real. How could folks worship and pray and obey all their lives and think otherwise? Still, he was amazed. Grandma Coffey's death seemed to connect him to the other world, the paradise he couldn't see. He was so thankful to Grandma Coffey. He did not fear death, and he trusted God.

Billy's father recovered, his sad face even more woeful. But inside he had changed.

One morning, Billy was amazed to see dozens of folks parking cars by the farmhouse as he left for school. The men from the club were gathering right in Frank Graham's pasture by a pine grove. They were going to pray all day long.

Their wives were walking to the house to spend the day praying with Mother. And they were all still there when Billy came home after school to start his chores.

That night his father was glowing. "What a day with the Lord! This fall we're going to build a tabernacle—"

"Tabernacle!" blurted out Billy.

"A huge house of worship with a steel frame and enclosed by pine boards," said his father firmly. "We're going to revive our faith in the Lord Jesus."

"A real old-time revival meeting?" asked Billy.

"Yes," said his father. "And we're going to get us a real old-time preacher who will revive our faith!"

Mother said, "I heard a man at your prayer meeting begged the Lord to let Charlotte give rise to a preacher who would spread the gospel to the ends of the earth!"

"I don't know who that preacher from Charlotte is going to be," laughed Billy, "but I'm sure it isn't going to be me." Not even his mother disagreed with him.

Billy was driving the family car to school. It was amazing how sporty the dark blue Plymouth sedan became when the driver had a nice tan face, wavy blond hair, and a dazzling smile. His interest in girls had advanced beyond talk. But doing more than kissing a girl outside of marriage was just unthinkable.

Billy reminded himself constantly with Scripture: "God is faithful, who will not suffer you to be tempted above that ye are able; but will with the temptation also make a way to escape, that ye may be able to bear it."

And God was faithful to Billy.

So Billy had two great interests: girls and baseball. He was sure he was a natural-born first baseman, with windmill arms that snapped balls out of the air like a bullfrog snapped flies. It was just a matter of time before he started connecting with the bat.

Milking cows had given him a grip that could make a grown man cry. And his long, farm-strong arms blurred the bat when he swung. If he hit the ball square, the ball soared into the sky. The problem was that he never hit it square, except in batting practice.

"You'll whack it someday," encouraged Melvin.

Mordecai Ham came to Charlotte late in the fall of 1934 to preach at the revival meetings Billy's father had talked about. But how would Billy find time to go? He was back in high school starting his junior year, and when he wasn't working on the farm, he played baseball. Or he talked to girls. But when Billy heard that Mordecai Ham had said the kids at the high schools in Charlotte were sinful, he found the time.

"I've got to hear this Dr. Ham for myself," Billy complained angrily. "Somebody's got to stand up for the honor of Charlotte's young people."

Billy went to the revival with Albert McMakin, a young man who had been in the tabernacle in downtown Charlotte before. The tabernacle built by the Christian Men's Club stunned Billy. He seemed transported into paradise. The immense interior was lit by dozens of high-swinging bulbs as sunny as angels. The air smelled of delicious pine from the sawdust that covered the ground. Hundreds of folks were already there, sitting on benches and crates and chairs. And there was room for many more.

"I want to be right down front," insisted Billy sticking his pointed chin farther out.

"No, you don't," said Albert in such a forceful way that Billy didn't argue.

So they sat in one of the back rows. "I never understand why folks sit at the back," grumbled Billy.

He really couldn't understand. Scared as he was when he first started school, he had sat down in the front row—silent, but all ears and eyes. Billy gawked around. "How many folks are coming, Albert?"

"Four thousand most nights."

The tabernacle slowly filled. Billy had never felt like he did that night. The tabernacle was a pulsing, living thing. There were so many people. And they seemed so eager to hear the Word of the Lord. Were folks so thirsty for the living water?

Mordecai Ham appeared on the stage. He was about fifty years old, with a thin white mustache and only a fringe of white hair above his ears. He wore rimless glasses on a pasty white face.

Billy was disappointed. How was this colorless man going to take on a crowd of four thousand? Billy sat up tall so he wouldn't miss anything. He hoped the colorless Mordecai Ham spoke loud enough. Would this insignificant preacher dare repeat his slurs against the students at the Charlotte high schools?

As Billy watched, Mordecai Ham's pale face grew redder. "You are a sinner!" bellowed Mordecai Ham. He pointed right at Billy!

"Me?" gasped Billy. He slumped in his chair. How did Mordecai Ham know about him chasing girls? Mordecai Ham preached on and on about sin. Before the evening was over, Billy really knew he was a sinner. How ignorant he had been about revivalists. Mordecai Ham had thrashed Billy and 3,999 other souls from the tops of their heads to their toenails!

Billy went back to the meetings again and again. He had never heard or seen anyone who could preach like Mordecai Ham. He had heard some pretty good preachers over the radio. But in person, with all his senses tuned in, this preaching shook Billy's soul.

But Billy made sure he never sat in Mordecai Ham's line of fire again. He joined the choir, which stood behind the preacher. He was next to a boy his same age, Grady Wilson.

Grady liked to tease. "Billy, you sing worse than a calf bawling for its mama."

Billy did not care if Grady Wilson knew he couldn't sing or not. He was not going to be the target of Mordecai Ham again.

Every night Mordecai Ham ended his preaching by calling folks to the altar to accept Jesus as their Savior and be born again.

One night after Mordecai Ham invited sinners to the altar, Billy felt the presence of the living Christ. Was Jesus telling him to go to the altar? Billy resisted. He was already a Christian. He was baptized. Of course he didn't remember being baptized. He was just a baby. But he was Christian. Wasn't he?

Billy glanced at Grady Wilson. Grady was very troubled.

"I thought I was already saved," he stammered. "Maybe I'm not." Grady lurched forward to the altar.

What if Billy's own soul wasn't saved? Would he wait until it was too late to be saved?

Billy found himself stumbling awkwardly to the altar. Then his father was suddenly beside Billy, tears in his eyes. Sad-faced Daddy had wanted Billy to be born again all along and had never once pestered him about it. God would make it happen or not happen. And God made it happen.

"I'm a changed boy," Billy told his mother that evening.

But in his bedroom later that night, to the sound of Melvin snoring, Billy felt all his flaws magnified. He wanted to feel righteous, but he felt like a great sinner. Maybe he didn't really understand what living in Christ meant.

Weeks later, his mother said, "You've calmed down, Billy. I know you have always loved other people, but you didn't slow down long enough to let them know it."

Billy had changed. He was very conscious of sin. And not everyone appreciated it. He'd started meddling with kids at school, telling them right out if they did something wrong. So he stopped.

But some kids started calling Billy and Grady Wilson the Preacher Boys, anyway. And they were not teasing. Billy was learning that some folks wanted their religion watered down or not at all. If it reminded them of their sins, they became very angry.

"Blessed am I when people persecute me because of

Jesus," Billy reminded himself. "That's what the Bible says." But it hurt deep inside because Billy liked everyone. And it was very hard to pray for persecutors like the Bible said. But he did.

Billy began preaching to the children on the farm. Once Billy had dreamed of being lord of the jungle like Tarzan. Later he'd dreamed of playing baseball in the major leagues like Babe Ruth. Now he dreamed of mastering thousands of sinners under a big tent. "Come down and be saved," he would cry, and thousands flocked to the altar—in his imagination.

I wonder if I could really do that? he asked himself. He remembered how poorly he gave oral reports in school.

Then he heard Grady Wilson was going to preach inside a real church! Grady was just a senior in high school like Billy. Billy went to listen.

Before the sermon, Grady asked Billy, "Can you loan me your watch, buddy? I've got to be careful, so I allow enough time for my whole sermon."

Billy loaned Grady his watch and sat down in a pew with Grady's girlfriend. He was amazed when Grady began preaching. Grady was really good. Billy thought, *That's my buddy Grady up there. Plain as mud. Why can't I do that, too?*

All during the sermon, Grady's eyes darted down at Billy's watch, and he kept winding the stem. He had to make sure the watch kept running. After the sermon, Grady handed Billy his watch. "I'm sorry about the watch, buddy. But you shouldn't have held hands with my girl. It made me kind of anxious."

Billy just had to laugh. Grady always made him laugh. Besides, he was so amazed that Grady could preach he didn't even mind that Grady had wound the stem right off his watch. If plain-as-mud Grady could preach, why couldn't Billy?

On the farm, the family started talking about Billy becoming a preacher, too. "Maybe Billy will be that preacher from Charlotte who spreads the gospel to the ends of the world," said Mother.

"God willing." Billy's father looked pained to presume such a thing.

"Grady Wilson is going out west to Tennessee to that Bible college run by Dr. Bob Jones," volunteered Billy.

"I never heard of it," said Mother.

"What's it cost?" asked his father.

"Well now, you know Grady couldn't afford much, Daddy."

"That's it, then. It's Bob Jones," said his father, looking like he could make no better bargain than that.

Suddenly Billy was out of high school with a diploma in his hand. Albert McMakin had left Charlotte to sell Fuller brushes door-to-door in South Carolina. He invited Billy to come and sell brushes with him that summer. Grady Wilson would join them, too.

"But I thought you were going to help me on the farm this summer," said Billy's father.

"I can save up money for college this way, Daddy," gushed Billy.

"Don't worry, Frank. He'll be back in two weeks," scoffed an onlooker.

On that discouraging note, Billy left with Grady Wilson to go to South Carolina. The very first time Billy tried selling, he opened his case of brushes, found one of his cheapest Fuller brushes, and knocked on the door of his potential customer. The door opened. An exasperated face appeared in the doorway. "Yes?"

"I'm Billy Graham, Ma'am. Your Fuller Brush man. I'd like to give you a free brush today." He held out the brush. "All you have to—"

"Thanks, Sonny." The woman snatched the brush out of his hands and slammed the door.

"Say, wait just a cotton-picking minute!" Billy stared at the solid door. He never even got a chance to smile.

He learned fast. At the next house, Billy said the same words, smiling pure sunshine. But he took his sweet time digging though hair brushes and toothbrushes and clothes brushes for the free brush. Never again did a customer get a free brush without hearing an unstoppable avalanche of words. And Billy made sure his customer was blinded by his smile.

Like everything Billy did outside of school, he threw himself into it heart and soul. He really did believe his brushes were the best in the world, and no housewife could survive without them. He began to sell brushes left and right. And only later, when he stopped to think about it, was he amazed, because while he was selling, he never doubted for a moment he was going to sell every brush in his case.

Albert McMakin was amazed, too. "You're selling more brushes than I am, Billy."

After a few weeks, Billy was making as much money as a man with a real job. But he didn't save much of it. Billy liked nice clothes, and he bought himself suits and hand-painted ties. And of course a salesman needed several pairs of comfortable shoes—nice saddle shoes, too, not clogs. One thing was for sure. At the end of summer, Billy would have a mighty fine wardrobe.

One Sunday afternoon in Monroe, North Carolina, a preacher-friend named Jimmy Johnson took Billy and Grady Wilson to a jail. Facing cells full of grumbling prisoners, most of whom were recovering from a wild Saturday night, Jimmy suddenly pointed at Billy. "I have a young fellow here who was just recently saved. Give our friends your testimony, Billy."

Billy was so surprised he dropped his case full of brushes. He froze. Preaching terrified him. He began to nervously wring his yellow-trimmed green suit coat he had taken off because the jail was so hot and sticky.

Jimmy was amused. It was an old trick on would-be preachers.

Help me, Lord, prayed Billy. Hadn't he practiced a hundred million times? *Get me started, Lord,* he prayed.

"I'm glad to see so many of you came out to hear me

today," said Billy, remembering. He heard Grady cackle with glee. Billy screamed, "I was a sinner!" He was talking to God now. Did he hear a weak "Amen" drift from a cell?

"I was no good!" He punched the air. "I forgot God!" Another weak "Amen, Brother" seemed to drift out of a dark, sweltering cell.

Billy began to walk around and punch the air with his suit coat as he spat out his testimony in short sentences. "I didn't care about God! I didn't care about people!" He hunched over, then shot straight up with each sentence. Always the arms flailed.

"Finally I accepted Jesus!" His voice bounced off the walls, each word as loud and clear as a church bell. A few more "Amens" made him louder yet. "Jesus brought me joy!"

How long he talked, Billy didn't know. He could hear "Amens" roll out of the cells after every sentence. The prisoners were responding! He felt like he could fly. Finally he stopped, trembling, in a state of joy he had never felt before. It would be a good while before the excitement wore off.

"So that's what preaching is really like," he gushed to Grady later. And Grady seemed amazed by what Billy had done.

After summer was over, Billy's father drove the boys out west to Bob Jones's Bible college in Tennessee. Billy had a plan to get himself and Grady elected officers in the freshman class. Billy nominated Grady for president of the class.

Grady won the election. But when it came time for Grady to nominate Billy for an office, they found out officers couldn't nominate candidates.

"Thanks, Buddy," said President Grady Wilson afterward, as innocent as an angel. "The first part of your plan was brilliant."

Billy got even at the talent show. He talked Grady into singing a duet. Grady frowned. "Are you sure? I don't want to hurt your feelings, but you sing worse than a lovesick hound dog, Billy."

As Grady stood up after being announced to sing, he suddenly realized he was standing alone. He managed to croak through the song as Billy hunkered down in his seat.

When a fuming Grady returned to his seat, Billy tried to look as innocent as an angel. "You were right. I don't sing well enough. Thanks for sharing your wisdom with me, Buddy, before it was too late."

After a few weeks, Billy was unhappy because of the strict rules at the college. Boys couldn't talk to girls. Every letter in or out was read by school officials. For the first time in Billy's life, he had trouble sleeping.

When he returned home for Christmas vacation, everyone thought Billy had the flu because he was so miserable. He had to be dragged along in his father's new green Plymouth when the Grahams drove south to visit his mother's sister in Florida. But at each gasoline stop as they drove deeper into Florida, Billy began to be the first one out of the car.

"So this is Florida," he muttered and gawked. "It's warm for December."

By the time they neared Orlando, he was leaping from the car. "Look at the palm trees!" His arms spread out. "Look. Flowers everywhere!" He flailed his arms. "Feel that balmy air." He punched the air. "Can this be December?" He clapped his hands. "What a paradise!"

After they visited Billy's aunt in Orlando, the Graham family took a side trip. Near Tampa, in the midst of orange groves, the Grahams stopped to survey the Florida Bible Institute.

Pale stucco buildings with red-tiled roofs overlooked tennis courts and a sprawling golf course. Nearby, the Hillsboro River crept along under cypress trees with moss hanging from their limbs.

"It's beautiful," gushed Billy.

His mother said casually, "It's a fine institution to study God's Word. I read about it in *Moody Monthly*." Then Billy recalled hearing about this Florida school before. How grateful he was to his mother. He daydreamed of striding across campus in bright sunshine, glowing in his lime-colored suit and hot pink tie, free to talk to any pretty girl he saw.

Two months later, Billy's father drove him back to the Florida Bible Institute. Billy's only regret was that Grady couldn't afford the school.

Billy soon learned many preachers—or evangelists— came to vacation and lecture there because the institute maintained part of the hotel for that very purpose. Students carried luggage, caddied golf, waited tables, washed dishes, and met veteran evangelists.

Billy drank in their lectures. He sat wide-eyed and gulped down their informal discussions, too. One name kept emerging as a giant: Billy Sunday.

Billy Sunday had been everything Billy Graham wanted to be. He had been a major league baseball player. At the age of 28, he'd had his best season ever with 123 hits and 84 stolen bases—the most stolen bases in one season until Ty Cobb topped the record many years later. Sunday was paid more in one month than most men made in one year. And suddenly he quit baseball to evangelize for Christ!

Old evangelists explained how Billy Sunday used the pulpit like a stage actor, with a leather-lunged voice and exaggerated gestures to capture the farthest listener. He stomped his feet and pounded his fists. He raced across the platform and slid like he was sliding into a base. He screamed at "bull-necked, hog-jowled, weasel-eyed, sponge-spined, mush-fisted, yellow-livered, hell-bound sinners."

"How could anybody ever top Billy Sunday?" asked Billy Graham.

The warning was out at the institute: A student had to be ready to preach at all times. Billy polished four sermons until he had what he figured to be at least two hours of preaching in his heart. Who knew when he would be called?

John Minder, a dean at the school and the director of the

Tampa Gospel Tabernacle, took Billy with him on Easter vacation to Jacksonville. And sure enough, Billy got his call: He was going to preach that very night in Bostwick, a small town near Jacksonville!

About thirty people were in the congregation that night. Billy got wound up and hammered out all four sermons in less than ten minutes. The experienced Dean Minder easily filled in the remaining time. But Billy felt miserable. Why couldn't he slow down and preach like a real preacher?

When they returned to school, Dean Minder asked Billy to be the youth director at the Tampa Gospel Tabernacle.

"Me?" asked Billy, still bothered by his experience in Bostwick.

"Our youth group is small and discouraged, and you're just the man to pep them up."

Billy threw himself into the new job with his usual energy. The teens in Tampa were seeking God. They responded to Billy's loud, arm-waving prayers. The group grew larger. Billy was thrilled that he could lead. Maybe he was cut out to serve God after all.

Not all his experiences in Florida were warm glowing ones. Once in Tampa, Billy saw a man hit by a car. The man writhed and screamed that he was lost, slipping to hell. What could be more frightening than eternity in hell? Any time Billy weakened in his efforts, he would think of that man lying on the brink of eternal torture. Eternal hell.

Night after night, Billy lay awake in his dorm room,

tormented by his doubts. Was he really meant to preach? Sometimes he got up to wander the grounds, even roaming the spongy fairways of the golf course. He brooded on and on, unable to sleep, wandering in lonely misery.

Help me, God, he prayed.

On one cool night in the spring of 1938, Billy sat down on the eighteenth green, facing the dark sloping fairway. Suddenly the doubt lifted. Flickering through his mind were images of rallies, throngs of folks spread before a platform higher than a throne. He knew in his heart that somehow he was going to be a small part of that vision.

Billy got on his knees. "The first commandment is to love the Lord my God with all my heart and with all my soul and with all my mind. I surrender, Lord! If You want me to spread the gospel by preaching, I will!"

Billy threw himself into his relationship with Christ. He prayed for hours on end. He read the Bible as he never had before. He was appointed assistant pastor of the Tampa Gospel Tabernacle.

That was not enough. Billy became the preacher to a trailer park. He preached to Cuban-Americans through an interpreter. He preached on the student radio station. He stalked the streets of Tampa. No sinner was safe. Once when Billy preached on a sidewalk in downtown Tampa, a man whacked him sprawling into the street.

"It is an honor to suffer for Christ," said Billy, surveying the dirt on his suit like it was gold. He meant it. He really felt the Holy Spirit inside him.

But Billy still had doubts. He bounced around the pulpit, flailed the air with his arms like a man swatting flies, and boomed his raw North Carolina twang off the ceilings. He jabbed his finger. His message was plain vanilla: You are a sinner. Christ died to pay for your sins. But you must accept Christ to be saved.

Does God want me to preach this way? he asked himself. No one else preached so fast and furiously. *Results are what count, aren't they? Can I, or can I not, bring sinners to accept Christ and His salvation?* Billy had never called people to the altar after his sermon to accept Christ. The regular pastor did that.

There was only one way for Billy to get the answer. *I've got to test myself,* he resolved.

And he faced the test with fear and trembling.

When the night for his first altar call came, Billy gnawed his fingernails, sick with worry. He had prayed all afternoon for God's help. "I'll have to quit preaching if I fail," he glumly reminded himself. "If I can't bring folks to the altar to accept Christ, I'm just making a lot of noise."

One hundred people were in the congregation that night to listen to Billy preach. Heart thumping, he began. As he preached, he felt the Holy Spirit helping him. Arms flailing and words exploding like gunfire, he delivered the gospel. But at the end of his sermon, his heart was in his mouth.

"Now, friends, if you want your life to change tonight," he said, "come forward now and accept Christ as your Savior." His mouth was dry as desert sand. Had his loud preaching turned people away from Christ?

Hands clasped, eyes down, Billy waited in sweaty humility. Surely at least one person would come. *Oh please, God, just one.* All he wanted was one. If only he could lead one sinner to Jesus. Billy waited. What if no one came?

Slowly, a man stood up. Was the man going to come to the altar, or was he simply leaving the church? The man hesitated. Sin was so hard to acknowledge publicly. The man slowly turned to the altar. Yes! He was coming forward. Oh, praise the Lord!

Another person stood up. Could it be that she was coming to Christ, too? Or was she leaving? She came forward. Oh, yes. Praise the Lord.

Then another. And another.

Soon, people were rising so fast Billy could no longer count. He wanted to weep. He wasn't worthy of this. *Oh, rebuke me, God,* he prayed. *This was not my sermon. It was not my personal charm. God forgive me for even thinking that. The sinners are coming to Christ because the Holy Spirit was working through me.*

"Thirty-two came to the altar," said one member of the church later. "In all my years, I never saw so many come to the altar in one meeting. You have something special, Billy Graham."

By early 1940, Billy was close to graduating from the institute. What was he going to do then? In the meantime he was still a student, doing all the chores students did. One day he was caddying for two golfers named Elmer Edman and Paul Fisher.

Paul Fisher said, "We're from Wheaton, Illinois."

Billy gushed, "Where Wheaton College is located? What a coincidence. My mother always dreamed of me going there, but we couldn't afford it."

Fisher set his jaw. "I'll pay your room and board for one year."

Elmer Edman said, "And I'll pay your tuition for a year. After that, I expect you can get a scholarship. The truth is, we want Wheaton College to graduate Billy Graham."

"So we can claim you," said Fisher.

"If that doesn't beat all. Me?" said Billy. "Mother will be so happy."

So Billy went to Wheaton College in 1940. But he eyed Europe nervously. The continent was in the murderous grip of the Germans, corrupted by Adolf Hitler and his evil Nazi party. Would America have to fight the Germans?

Billy arrived at Wheaton College nearly twenty-two years old and an ordained minister, yet a mere freshman. He was a curiosity at first, the gangly, smiley southerner in his summery suits and bright ties. But all he had to do was lead one prayer in a student meeting, and those present never looked at him the same way again.

Billy met Ruth Bell. She was the daughter of missionaries in China. Dark-haired, she had sharp features and thin lips, but her face was softened by amber eyes, a creamy complexion, and complete innocence. Most girls gawked at Billy, but not Ruth. She hardly looked at him.

Billy immediately fell in love with her. He thought about her all the time. So he nervously invited her to a performance of *Messiah*. It seemed an eternity before she accepted!

Ruth was a perfect spiritual mate for Billy. The problem was that Ruth wanted to be a missionary. The more Billy thought about Ruth Bell, the more troubled he became. How could her goals ever be reconciled with his own goals? Could he rob this godly woman of her destiny? He backed off. Let God decide.

Many weeks later, Billy received a letter from Ruth: an invitation to a party. *So it is God's will,* he told himself.

Over the months, they saw each other often. Ruth was saintly. Her worn Bible had notes penciled in all the margins. She loved animals like Billy did. Animals were God's creatures. Ruth couldn't find a dead bird without burying it. To think of that precious creature lying out in the open made her sick.

Billy had never met anyone as fascinating as Ruth. She added a new dimension to his life. Longing for her gnawed at him constantly. Finally he decided he would ask Ruth to marry him and let God sort their careers out. Let God's will be done.

Billy asked Ruth to marry him. Ruth accepted and a little while later visited the Graham family in Charlotte, wearing her engagement ring. Billy's father was pleased with Billy's choices for both a wife and a calling. He said, "Some folks are saying the night Mordecai Ham snatched up Billy here for Christ was the very same night Billy Sunday died. . . ."

Billy was shocked. "Daddy, you never told me that before."

"I'm not sure it's true. Anyway, that's what some folks are saying."

"The great Billy Sunday. Imagine," mumbled Billy.

On December 7, 1941, the calm on the campus at Wheaton College exploded. Japanese planes had bombed the American naval base at Pearl Harbor in the Pacific Ocean. The next day, America declared war on Japan, and three days later, America declared war on Germany. World War II had begun for America!

Billy wanted to enlist as a soldier. Professors talked him out of it. Could he kill another man? If he couldn't, he was only endangering his fellow soldiers. So Billy tried to enlist as a chaplain, a man of God. The army told him he not only had to finish his college work first, but he also needed one year as a full pastor to qualify as a chaplain.

In 1943, Billy graduated from Wheaton College. He was offered a pastorship in nearby Western Springs, Illinois. The small basement church of thirty-five members was barely surviving, but Billy was undaunted. He could hardly wait to get started as a real pastor.

Yet he had another great event in his life to take care of first. After three years of courtship, Billy married Ruth at Montreat, North Carolina, where Ruth's parents lived.

When the Billy Grahams returned to Illinois, Billy began pastoring at Western Springs. The members were stunned by his sin-prodding, machine-gun delivery. But more and more people joined the church. And most important, Billy persuaded them to come to the altar to accept Christ.

"You really do have the power of the Holy Spirit," said Ruth in awe.

Billy was awed, too, when he had time to stop and reflect. But he stayed very busy. It seemed almost overnight that he started a prayer group of prominent businessmen. He welcomed their donations to his church because the money could do so much toward spreading the gospel.

Opportunities seemed to seek Billy out. They found him because he was everywhere, opening doors. One day he was approached with an offer from Torrey Johnson, another pastor. Billy rushed home to Ruth with news of Pastor Johnson's offer. This opportunity seemed a hundred times greater than anything before.

"Torrey Johnson started too many activities," Billy explained to Ruth. "He has to cut back. He offered me his radio program. It's broadcast by WCFL—50,000 watts. My parents and your parents will hear me way down in North Carolina, especially since we broadcast late at night."

By the beginning of 1944, Billy was welcoming radio listeners to *Songs in the Night* from "the friendly church in the pleasant community of Western Springs." Following a hymn sung by Bev Shea, Billy burst in over a background of bad news with a sermon on the urgent need for Christ.

Billy had smoothed his twang into a honeyed southern accent. The radio program proved that Billy's power to persuade people wasn't from his blue eyes or his lion's mane of golden hair. He was very popular. Donations from listeners poured in to the church.

Torrey Johnson next asked Billy to help him with revival meetings. Billy was eager to help. First the revivals were for soldiers in the Chicago area. Then they expanded to all the young people around Chicago. Finally the meetings were for young people nationwide.

Suddenly Billy was preaching to crowds of ten thousand! It happened so fast that he never had a chance to be overwhelmed by what he was doing. Torrey Johnson had him traveling all over America, making arrangements for future rallies of Youth for Christ.

By early 1945, Billy was so busy with Torrey Johnson's rallies that he could no longer do his radio program or even pastor his church. Ruth urged him to choose. Was Billy going to be a traveling evangelist or a pastor of a church? She thought it was impossible to be both. Billy chose evangelism. Ruth was happy with his choice.

Preaching and planning rallies for teens meant Billy had to travel constantly. Ruth missed him but joked she would rather have a little of Billy than a lot of anybody else. She left Illinois to live with her parents in Montreat, North Carolina.

Billy understood. People serving Christ had to make sacrifices. Besides, America was at war, and President Franklin Roosevelt had died suddenly. Billy not only mourned the dead president but prayed for his successor, Harry Truman.

One month later the Germans surrendered. By September, the Japanese had surrendered, and World War II was over. Over ten million young Americans returned from the war to resume their lives.

Ruth gave birth to their daughter Virginia on September 21. Ruth nicknamed her "GiGi," Chinese for sister.

The Youth for Christ movement had become such a national sensation that President Truman praised it. *Time* magazine ran a story on it. The newspaper empire of William Randolph Hearst assigned one reporter full-time to cover the movement.

The Youth for Christ organization got local clergy to counsel those who came to Christ. That made a revival much more effective but also much more difficult to plan. Advance planning became a very big job—and it was Billy's.

Torrey Johnson decided it was time Youth for Christ became international. The team that left for England included Torrey Johnson and Billy.

The English were shocked by Billy. They had no pastors who preached in bright red bow ties and pink suits. Their pastors did not stalk the platform, bending down, bolting upright, flailing their arms. They had no pastors who spoke at the rate of 240 words per minute and never used an adjective or adverb.

Billy's simple message of sin and salvation spattered the audience like machine gunfire. There was no escape. Most stunning of all to the English was the stream of sinners coming to the altar to accept Christ after Billy called them.

Back in America, anticipation of a series of revival meetings for Youth for Christ in Charlotte created one of Billy's black moments of doubt. What if he failed in his own backyard?

"We've got to go all out for Charlotte," he said nervously to Ruth.

Billy chewed his nails. He spurred an advance campaign

that went far beyond the usual billboards, bumper stickers, radio commercials, and placards in buses and windows. Billy had airplanes zooming over Charlotte, trailing banners, and dropping leaflets. He gave daily press releases to thirty-one local newspapers. He hired variety acts.

Billy hired Cliff Barrows, Bev Shea, and his old buddy Grady Wilson. Grady was married now, with his own ministry in South Carolina. He was still just as quick-witted and sharp-tongued as ever. He knew how to keep Billy's feet on the ground. Billy loved Grady.

Yet Billy still had doubts. *Lord, don't let me fail in my own backyard.*

Billy's revival meetings at Charlotte drew forty-two thousand people. As usual, if people could be gathered, Billy could persuade many of them to come to Christ.

The team of Billy, Cliff Barrows, Bev Shea, and Grady Wilson worked well together. Grady was Billy's jack-of-all-trades. He could organize prayer groups, preach if Billy got sick, tell funny stories, or cook breakfast. Burly song leader Cliff, swinging his trombone, bounced through the singing like a cheerleader. Dignified Bev preceded Billy's sermon with a hymn to set a serious tone.

So Billy's black moment had become one of his greatest leaps forward. He felt so good about his team that he wanted to go out on his own to evangelize.

In Montreat, Billy bought a house across the street from Ruth's parents. In May 1948, another daughter was born: Anne.

Billy drew away from the Youth for Christ organization more and more. He wanted to offer salvation to people of all ages. Finally he went on his own.

In 1949, Billy had his biggest test yet. For three weeks, his organization hoped to pack six thousand people, six nights a week and twice on Sunday, into Billy's Canvas Cathedral—a huge, three-spired circus tent in downtown Los Angeles.

The campaign had the support of local churches as well as the mayor and local celebrities like Stuart Hamblen, a singing Texan with a daily radio program. Most important to Billy's sense that all would go well was the presence of his team: Grady Wilson, Cliff Barrows, and Bev Shea.

Since they now embraced a wider audience than just teens, Billy toned down the service so that it was more a church service and less of a colorful show. His gaudy clothing was gone. He usually wore dark suits.

Clutching his black Bible, Billy would borrow an old-time evangelist's phrase and bellow, "The Bible says," and go on to quote Scripture. Then he would begin to condemn those who disobeyed God's Word and explain the dreaded consequences: everlasting hell.

Billy wore a microphone on the lapel of his coat so he could be heard in the farthest corners of the tent. He still stalked the platform, cracking out words in a honeyed southern accent like pops of lightning. He locked his eyes on several hundred sinners at once.

When he had thousands of them squirming, it was time for

a change of pace. He would soften his tone for awhile. Billy hammered through the list of sins: love of material things, alcoholism, adultery, suicide, stealing, cheating, greed.

No one was safe. The radio star Stuart Hamblen, who had a reputation for wild living, quickly found that out. Billy pistoled his finger in Hamblen's direction and snapped, "There's a man in here leading a double life!" The next night he leveled his finger at Hamblen again: "There's a phony in here tonight!" After that night Hamblen refused to attend.

The local committee asked Billy if he wanted to extend the revival beyond three weeks. Billy had never extended a revival before, no matter how successful, because he always had others planned. But this time was different.

"I'll ask for a sign from God," Billy said nervously, "like Gideon did in the Book of Judges when he put out a fleece. Gideon had to know if God wanted him to do a certain thing, so one night he put a sheepskin outside on the ground. If in the morning the fleece was covered with dew, yet the ground around it was completely dry, that would be a sign from God to go ahead. And God gave Gideon the sign to go ahead: The fleece was wet."

"But what will be your sign, Billy?" asked one of the team.

"I don't know," he admitted nervously.

CHAPTER 5

Billy got a phone call from Stuart Hamblen in the middle of the night. He wanted to repent of his sins and accept Christ. Hamblen's change of heart was miraculous, surely a sign from God to continue the revival in Los Angeles.

"Please, Lord, help Stuart convert from sinner to Your faithful servant," prayed Billy.

On his radio program, Hamblen announced he had repented, promising to give up alcohol, cigarettes, even all his racehorses—except El Lobo, who was like a family pet. After several days, Stuart's decision to become a servant of Christ seemed real.

Not long after that success, Louis Zamperini came to the altar. Zamperini had been a world-class distance runner and a hero in World War II, but finally his great courage failed him. Until Billy brought him to Christ, he tried to find courage in a whiskey bottle.

Success snowballed. Another man came to the altar. He was a crook for a notorious Los Angeles gangster. Curious Hollywood celebrities began to attend the revivals to see who was salvaging all these fallen men.

Suddenly the revival was being touted in the Los Angeles newspapers of William Randolph Hearst, with full-page stories and photos of Billy preaching to the crowd like John the

Baptist. A few days later, reporters from the national magazines *Life, Newsweek,* and *Time* showed up.

"That's wonderful," gushed Billy.

But Billy was exhausted. *Fatigue is a tool of the devil,* he told himself. "The more tired I become physically, the stronger I must become spiritually," he declared, echoing the apostle Paul.

Finally, on November 20, the tent meetings came to an end. For that last meeting, the crowd overflowed the Canvas Cathedral into the street, blocking traffic. In eight weeks in Los Angeles, Billy had drawn 350,000 listeners!

"It will be kind of nice to get away from all the hubbub for awhile," said Billy as he boarded the train to go east the next day.

But the train was no refuge. Billy was amazed to discover that everyone seemed to know him. At Kansas City, reporters rushed inside the train, rudely asking questions and taking photographs. He wanted to tell them to back off, but wouldn't he be betraying his friends? Wasn't this the publicity the revival movement needed?

Billy followed Los Angeles with revivals in Boston and South Carolina. They were successful, too. At the University of South Carolina, Billy filled the football stadium with forty thousand people hungry for Christ. Ten thousand had to be turned away. It was the first time he called his revival a crusade.

Word of his successful crusades spread like wildfire to

the highest circles of the country. Billy was invited to pray before the United States Congress in Washington, D.C.

Billy was increasingly nervous about success. It was all so much, so fast. Would he falter? He had to remind himself that Billy Graham wasn't going to succeed or falter. His success was God's success. But the reporters kept turning it into Billy Graham's success. And he had to keep repeating, "No, no, this is God's glory."

Billy was determined not to take credit for his success. He believed that if he did, his power would end as suddenly as it had for Moses when he struck the rock at Kadesh.

In Billy's experience, people suffered from four miseries: emptiness, loneliness, guilt, and fear of death. Unless he was aiming at a specific audience like teenagers and how they could enlist Christ to fight sexual temptation, he would preach on one of those main four human miseries. Of course, the answer to these miseries was Christ.

During the call to the altar, Billy would plant his chin in his right hand, reminding himself that people were responding to the Holy Spirit, not to Billy Graham. And yet when people came forward, Billy tried to look every one of them in the eye. Who could know if that extra encouragement might make their conversion just a little stronger? They were babes in Christ. They had to be encouraged in every way.

He said the "sinner's prayer" with them: "Oh God, I am a sinner. I'm sorry for my sins. I'm willing to turn from my sins. I receive Christ as my Savior. I confess Him as my

Lord. From this moment on I want to follow Him and serve Him in the fellowship of the church. In Christ's name, amen."

Then volunteers from local churches counseled the new believers in Christ on what to do next.

After one crusade, Billy received an invitation. He was stunned. He asked Grady, "What do we have scheduled for July 14, 1950?"

"Let me see."

"Never mind. Cancel it. We've been invited to the White House."

Grady was excited. "The White House? To meet President Truman? How should we dress?"

"What do you mean?" asked Billy. "Wear a dark suit and black shoes."

"But Truman is a very casual guy. Haven't you seen pictures of him in Florida at Key West in his spiffy white buck shoes and colorful Hawaiian shirts?"

"We can't wear Hawaiian shirts to the White House," argued Billy.

"What about white bucks?"

"That would definitely break the ice," enthused Billy. "We could wear light summer suits, hand-painted ties, and white buck shoes. We'll let the president know we're down-to-earth folks—just like he is."

And that's how Billy, Cliff Barrows, and Grady Wilson dressed for the White House. The president greeted them, standing ramrod straight in a dark suit. After they chatted a few minutes, Billy ended the meeting with a prayer. Reporters flocked around Billy as he left the White House. He was very pleased with his meeting. He told them what had been said.

The next day one of the team told Billy, "The newspaper says we really goofed. We shouldn't have talked about what was said in the meeting. The president is real mad about it."

"Oh Lord, how puffed up we were," said Billy, remembering.

"My son, despise not the chastening of the LORD; neither be weary of his correction," quoted Ruth. "Isn't that one of your favorite verses?" she added not so innocently.

"Proverbs 3:11," confirmed Billy. "Amen. God yanked us up short and booted us right in the seat of our pants!"

Billy moved on to his Portland crusade. It was difficult for him to walk about freely. People swarmed all around him as if he were a celebrity. He spent more and more time in his hotel room when he wasn't preaching. He would remain in his room, dressed very casually, wearing a green baseball cap to keep his unruly hair matted down, until he finally left to preach in the afternoon or evening.

Things were happening at a feverish pace. On November 5, 1950, Billy launched his new weekly radio program across the entire nation. The program opened with the stirring "Battle Hymn of the Republic," followed by Cliff Barrows who finished his introduction with: "This is the *Hour of Decision!*"

Then Grady Wilson would read a passage from the Bible,

and Bev Shea would sing a hymn. Next Billy would relate current news items to the Bible. Then relentlessly, never faltering once for a word, he warned his listeners of impending hell without Christ.

At his crusade in Atlanta, Billy met the widow of the great evangelist Billy Sunday. Ma Sunday, as she was called, had some bitter advice.

"Boys," she said, "I know you have to travel night and day to spread the gospel. It's the Great Commission in the last chapter of the book of Matthew. But don't let your wives neglect your kids. I thought I had to travel all over the country with Billy Sunday. We trashed the lives of our own kids." Tears streamed down her face.

Billy had felt very guilty about leaving Ruth behind in North Carolina with GiGi and Anne. Because of Ma Sunday's torment, he would never feel guilty again. But he would miss Ruth and his children very much when he was gone.

Billy formed a corporation because so much money was pouring in. That way he could account for every penny that was donated. It was very important that people know he wasn't getting rich from their donations. His organization was called the Billy Graham Evangelistic Association, or just BGEA.

With weekly radio programs and never ending citywide crusades, the demands on Billy's organization were great. The headquarters of BGEA in Minneapolis, Minnesota, added people to write scripts and take care of a thousand details. And if 1950 wasn't busy enough, Ruth gave birth to their third daughter on December 19. The infant Ruth was nicknamed "Bunny."

In 1950, Billy had begun a film company, too, one that would later be called World Wide Pictures. And since more and more Americans owned television sets, he felt the need to start a weekly television show called *Hour of Decision*.

"I learned long ago to open as many doors as possible," he reminded critics. He wasn't going to neglect any promising approach to spreading the gospel.

Billy's citywide crusades were changing for the better. He had stopped asking for offerings. His radio and television shows caused money to pour in to BGEA in Minneapolis, where every penny was carefully accounted for.

One ironclad requirement for a citywide crusade was that a majority of the local churches had to invite his crusade. That way Billy knew the city really wanted it and would furnish plenty of volunteers to counsel all those who came to the altar to accept Christ.

But another urgent need was gnawing at him.

CHAPTER 6

Billy always called people to the altar together, declaring pointedly, "The ground is level at the foot of the cross. I want all white folks, all black folks to come forward together."

In 1951, in many parts of America, white people still kept the races separate in schools and on buses and in other ways. Billy knew separating the races was not in Christ's teachings. But he thought white folks had to be won over gradually to allow integration.

Billy wasn't a hypocrite. It was the same way he handled prejudice against himself. He never tore into people because they criticized him or let him down. He approached them with love and friendly persuasion. But Billy knew blacks had to have equal justice and equal opportunities.

In 1952, Billy held a crusade in Washington, D.C. The Speaker of the House of Representatives, Sam Rayburn, praised him. "This country needs a revival, and I believe Billy Graham is bringing it to us."

With one nod from the powerful Speaker Rayburn, Billy gained what had seemed impossible: He got to hold his final rally on the steps of the Capitol! Billy had drawn over three hundred thousand people in five weeks. He made many friends among powerful politicians in both political parties. Among them were Lyndon Johnson and Richard Nixon.

Billy kept expanding his organization during 1952. In addition to his radio and television shows, he started a weekly newspaper column called "My Answer," in which he answered people's problems with Scripture. His family kept growing, too. Franklin was born July 14. The Grahams had four children. Ruth rarely traveled with Billy. One of the few times she did was on a trip to Korea.

America was involved in a war, trying to protect South Korea against the Communists of North Korea and China. Billy went to South Korea in late 1952. In a hospital, one severely wounded soldier, suspended face down in a contraption, begged to see Billy. So Billy crawled underneath to lie on the floor and pray with the soldier. Billy had seen some of the horror and heartbreak the soldiers knew. He prayed harder than ever for the war to end.

On the way back to America he told Ruth, "I feel like I went to Korea a boy and I'm coming back a man."

The Korean experience reminded Billy of another problem. Black soldiers were dying right beside white soldiers. When was the separation of races in some parts of America going to stop?

In March 1953, at his Chattanooga crusade, Billy declared, "Jesus Christ belongs neither to the black nor the white races. There are no color lines with Christ, as He repeatedly said that God looks upon the heart." Billy had to keep crusading to change the hearts of some prejudiced white people.

Even though Billy had not been appreciated by Harry

Truman, he did get off on the right foot with the man who'd just been elected the new president. Dwight Eisenhower was a World War II hero known to everyone as "Ike."

Billy gave Ike a red Bible. Ike seemed to really like Billy. He had asked Billy for advice on the speech he made after the ceremony in which he was sworn in as the new president.

In July 1953, the fighting in Korea stopped. Billy couldn't imagine a greater evil than godless communism. He thanked God that the fighting in Korea was over.

Next, he sat down with Ruth to write a book. Friends offered helpful criticism, and Billy and Ruth wrote the book again. Billy was very proud of the book. Surely this was God's doing.

He mailed it to a publisher in New York. The Doubleday Company published the book late in 1953. They named the book *Peace with God.*

"Can't we relax for awhile?" asked Ruth.

"We have a crusade in England." Billy's schedule seemed endless.

He drew such large crowds in England that his hosts set up a network of sites, with Billy's sermon relayed to each site by telephone. Each sermon was heard at over 400 churches and rented halls in 175 cities in Great Britain and Ireland. At each site, the local clergy talked to the audience before the sermon and counseled them afterward, just as they did in the arena where Billy preached.

At a London school, a student suddenly disrupted Billy's

sermon by leaping about and scratching like an ape.

"He reminds me of my ancestors," quipped Billy.

The students roared with laughter, sure the American evangelist had been caught admitting evolution was true, that people were descended from apes.

Billy added, "Of course, all my ancestors came from Great Britain."

On the last day of the crusade, Billy spoke to 120,000 people in Wembley Stadium. The day was such a success that the very formal and proper archbishop of Canterbury murmured, "I don't think we'll ever see a sight like this again until we get to heaven."

Grady Wilson gave the archbishop a bear hug and hooted, "That's right, Brother Archbishop! That's right!"

At noon on May 24, 1954, Billy found himself inside Number Ten Downing Street talking to none other than the British Prime Minister: the legendary Winston Churchill.

"Is there any hope for this world?" Churchill asked suddenly.

Billy was shocked. Was this the giant whose speeches gave the British people hope against the Nazi war machine in World War II? Or was he testing Billy?

Billy reached in his coat pocket and pulled out his New Testament. "Mr. Prime Minister, this fills me with hope!" And Billy punched out the message of Christ in his simple, direct way. Miraculously, Churchill allowed Billy to talk on and on. Before they parted, Billy assured him in prayer,

"God is the hope for the world you despair for."

Billy didn't tell reporters what he had talked about with Prime Minister Churchill. He only said that he felt like he had talked to "Mr. History."

In London, Billy had preached to two million people, either in person or by telephone relay.

In 1955, Billy was once again across the Atlantic Ocean, this time for his All-Scotland Crusade. The response night after night was so enthusiastic that the organizers telephoned broadcasts of the crusade into the rest of Great Britain and Ireland.

"Are you ready for the finale?" asked Grady, trying to act casual.

"If the Holy Spirit is," answered Billy nervously.

The meetings were going to end with the Good Friday meeting which BBC Television was televising to all of Britain. Only Queen Elizabeth's coronation had been watched by so many British people.

The day after Good Friday, people all over Britain were talking about Billy's sermon. Reviews were glowing. Later, he was allowed to preach privately to young Queen Elizabeth and her court at Windsor Castle.

President Eisenhower said that Billy Graham understood that "any advance in the world has got to be accompanied by a clear realization that man is, after all, a spiritual being."

In North Carolina, Ruth and the children were in a new home, Little Piney Cove, located on property Billy and Ruth had bought several years earlier. Ruth drove Billy in a Jeep along a winding road to their new home.

"Are you sure you want to be way up here on the mountain?" asked Billy.

"Ever since the trip to England in 1954, the tourists haven't left us alone. When I caught Bunny opening her small red purse to collect money from tourists in return for posing for pictures, I knew then and there we had to move!"

Now the Grahams had privacy in a large, U-shaped house constructed of logs Ruth had scrounged from old cabins. Below yawned a pine-covered valley. Above, clinging to the mountainside, thorny blackberry bushes fringed a forest of pine, aspen, and maple trees.

It rained often at Little Piney Cove. Soft rain seemed wonderful to Ruth; it depressed Billy. Because he fretted and gnawed his fingernails so much, the children dubbed him "Puddleglum," a lovable but pessimistic character in *The Silver Chair* by C. S. Lewis.

"Is the King dead? Has the enemy landed in Narnia?" giggled the children. GiGi was almost eleven, Anne eight, Bunny five, and Franklin three. They read all the Narnia books by C. S. Lewis.

In 1956, Billy helped Ruth's father, Nelson Bell, launch a new magazine. *Christianity Today* was one more improvement in the evangelistic machine Billy had built. He spread the gospel through crusades, movies, radio, television, a newspaper column, and a book. People had even named Billy's movement the "New Evangelicalism."

Billy said, "I believe that every word of the Bible is true and inspired by God. I believe God has existed forever as the Father, the Son, and the Holy Spirit. I believe Christ, born of a virgin, died for our sins, rose again, and will come again. I believe all people are sinners. I believe sinners can be saved only through accepting Christ as their Savior. These are beliefs held by all evangelicals. But if folks want to label me a New Evangelical, that's fine with me."

Billy never liked to quarrel.

In May 1957, Billy crusaded in New York. The results were staggering. Night after night in Madison Square Garden, Billy preached to nearly twenty thousand people.

Billy invited the Reverend Martin Luther King Jr., the black civil rights leader, to open one service in prayer. Billy wanted folks to see that whites and blacks work together for God. His comments in magazine interviews were more blunt: Hating anyone because of the color of his skin is a sin.

Nearing the end of sixteen weeks in New York, Billy had lost thirty pounds. " 'I can do all things through Christ which strengtheneth me,' " he said, quoting Philippians 4:13, one of his favorite verses. And he went on to draw one hundred thousand people into Yankee Stadium.

The last day of the New York crusade, Billy drew two hundred thousand people into Times Square. A grand total of 2.3 million people had attended the crusade.

"To God be all the glory," Billy told everyone. "This is His doing, and let no one fail to give Him the credit."

Then a confrontation held the attention of all America. The Arkansas governor was defying the Supreme Court's 1954 ruling that all public schools had to integrate. The Court had decided that officials couldn't keep black and white children in separate schools. The governor of Arkansas refused to allow black students to enter Central High School in Little Rock.

Billy got a phone call from the White House. Ike had been asking him for advice on racial matters. What did Billy think about Ike sending soldiers to Little Rock to force integration?

"Do it, Mr. President," advised Billy.

That afternoon, hard-nosed paratroopers of the 101st Airborne Division entered Little Rock. Central High School was integrated.

A second son, Nelson, was born January 12, 1958, and immediately dubbed "Ned." Billy continued to crusade.

That fall, white racists bombed a high school in Clinton, Tennessee. The school had just been integrated. Billy stepped forward to declare, "Every Christian should take his stand against these outrages."

In December, Billy spoke in Clinton to an audience of five thousand people to raise money for a new school, calling for "forgiveness, cool heads, and warm hearts."

One day in January 1959 when Billy was playing golf, he kept missing the ball. "The ground has ridges in it," he explained to Grady.

Grady chuckled. "Lord have mercy. That's a new excuse, Buddy."

Suddenly pain stabbed Billy's left eye.

At a clinic, doctors found that forty-year-old Billy had an eye disease. He was ordered to rest. But he could never be idle. He and Grady Wilson, along with their wives, studied the

Bible very hard as Billy rested.

"This is surely God's way of making me recharge my spiritual batteries," said Billy.

He established a routine for Bible reading that he hoped would stay with him forever. Every day he read five Psalms and a chapter of Proverbs so that he would read through both books every month. Proverbs instructed him on how to deal with other people. Psalms inspired him to talk to God. In addition Billy read enough of the rest of Scripture each day to get completely through the Bible once each year.

In 1959, Billy held very successful crusades in Australia and New Zealand. Back in America, Billy held two rallies in Little Rock. Racist groups mounted hate campaigns against him, but Billy, practicing the gospel of love, talked to everyone, trying to heal Little Rock of its bitterness. At the revivals, local pastors were stunned to see known white racists coming to the altar to repent of their sins and accept Christ. Little Rock was recovering.

In January 1960, Billy started to crusade through Africa. When he found out that blacks could not attend his rallies in the country of South Africa, he refused to go there.

At Kaduna, Nigeria, Billy was invited to visit a leper colony. He steeled himself against the sight of faces eaten away by the terrible disease. He preached to the residents, assuring them that God loved them and that a new spiritual body awaited them in heaven.

As he was about to leave, a small, maimed woman shuffled

toward him, extending an envelope with fingerless hands. It was a love offering from the people with leprosy for Billy's ministry.

"Boys," he told Grady and Cliff, "that's what the ministry is all about." Tears scalded his cheeks. This woman was like the widow in Luke 21, who gave two tiny copper coins—everything she had.

In America during the fall of 1961, Billy's crusade in Philadelphia included seven students from a seminary, a school for ministers. Why not let seminary students learn how to evangelize from the most effective evangelist in the world? After Philadelphia, the number of students, or interns, grew with every crusade.

Billy had always resisted the idea of his own school. "Maybe this is the form God wants my school to take: on-the-job training at the Billy Graham School of Evangelism."

In 1962, Billy was saddened by his seventy-four-year-old father's death. Billy didn't have to worry about his mother's financial security. Frank had quietly amassed a fortune. Not only had the dairy been profitable, but Frank's land had sprouted office buildings as the city of Charlotte grew and grew.

The following May, Billy's daughter GiGi married Stephan Tchividjian. Pleased, Billy told Ruth, "Many times I have prayed for such husbands for our daughters."

Nineteen sixty three was to be a year of turmoil. Blacks were going to jail, rallying in protest marches, and integrating

formerly all-white schools all over America. Billy supported their efforts. Some criticized him for wanting to go too
slow; some criticized him for wanting to go too fast.

But the most shocking event of 1963 took place in
November as Billy was playing golf near Montreat.

"Somebody shot at the president in a motorcade in
Dallas!" yelled someone.

"Surely not!" said Billy.

But President John Kennedy had been shot and killed.
Billy was sick. What a tragedy! Lyndon Johnson was sworn
in as the new president. Billy offered his services to
Johnson. Within one month, he was invited to the White
House for a fifteen-minute meeting.

Johnson's creased face showed terrible strain, and Billy
brought him the peace of God. Fifteen minutes became five
hours. They swam in the White House pool. Johnson relaxed
even more under Grady Wilson's endless barrage of jokes.

Billy cemented the friendship by telling reporters, "Lyndon Johnson is the most qualified man ever to take on the
presidency."

In 1964, Lyndon Johnson was reelected president. He
asked Billy to visit Selma, Alabama, where civil rights workers had been murdered. Billy also held a large integrated rally
in Birmingham, where a black church had been bombed.
Thirty-five thousand people, half black and half white, attended.

Billy supported Lyndon Johnson's new Great Society

programs, aimed at helping poor people of all races. But Billy was worried about something else. American soldiers were being sent to the far-off country of South Vietnam to fight Communist invaders.

Billy's crusade in the Astrodome in Houston was memorable because it was the first crusade a president attended. President Johnson and his wife, Lady Bird, flew over from their LBJ Ranch west of Austin for the final meeting.

Back in Montreat, Billy's daughter Anne married Danny Lotz. That winter Billy went to South Vietnam. He preached to the soldiers twenty-five times, often combining talents with comedian Bob Hope.

The situation in Vietnam was far worse than Billy had thought. Unless America threw its full might into the war, he saw no way to win and no way to get out. He acted as if he were optimistic, so the troops would not be discouraged. But he left convinced Vietnam was the most unfortunate foreign venture ever in America's long history.

CHAPTER 8

In 1967, Billy spent a lot of time with President Johnson. Many times he was a guest at Camp David, the White House, or the LBJ Ranch.

Pressured by President Johnson, Congress had passed many laws giving black Americans justice and equal rights. Yet President Johnson was very unpopular in America because of the war in Vietnam. And the war was crushing him. He took every American death in the war personally.

"The Johnson men do not live long," confided Johnson to Billy. In one very dark mood, he told Billy he wanted him to preach at his funeral. "Say something nice about me," he muttered.

In 1968, while Billy was in Australia, America turned topsy-turvy. President Johnson announced he would not run for president again. Days later Martin Luther King Jr. was killed by a sniper.

Things did not improve after Billy returned to America. Robert Kennedy was assassinated in Los Angeles, just as his brother John had been assassinated five years earlier in Dallas.

Billy was heartsick. He said, "America is going through its greatest crisis since the Civil War."

In the election for president, Richard Nixon squeaked out a narrow victory. President-elect Nixon asked Billy to say a prayer at his swearing-in ceremony in January. There was little doubt that President Nixon had a special regard for Billy. Richard Nixon was the first president to have a regular White House church service on Sunday morning. He asked Billy to preach the very first service.

In December 1968, Billy had been called to Walter Reed Hospital in Washington, D.C. Ike was dying. He had asked for Billy. They talked about eternity with God. Weeks later Ike was dead. An older era died with the old peacemaker.

Race and the war in Vietnam were burning issues in America. Billy continued to encourage those involved in the racial conflicts to cool off their tempers. He continued to give spiritual support to American troops in Vietnam.

Billy also continued his crusades. President Nixon spoke at Billy's crusade in Knoxville. Billy was delighted. It was so important to have the president openly testify about his faith in God.

"If only I could get President Nixon to call for a national day of repentance like Abraham Lincoln did!" cried Billy.

In 1969, Billy's daughter Bunny married Ted Dienert. Ruth was dealing with a rebellious Franklin, now seventeen. Several times she decided to win him over by showing him what a good sport she was. She hopped on his motorcycle, only to run it over an embankment once, into a lake once, and into a fence once.

Ruth was never the sophisticated socialite she appeared to be. She was more at home clubbing a rattlesnake on the mountain behind Little Piney Cove than clubbing a golf ball. Billy had always known that and loved her all the more for it.

In October 1971, Charlotte held a Billy Graham Day. President Nixon praised Billy. Billy liked Richard Nixon. He saw a warm side of the president that few people ever saw.

In 1973, Billy's old friend Lyndon Johnson died of a heart attack on almost the same day as the war in Vietnam stopped! It was as if the former president could at last rest in peace. As he'd promised, Billy spoke at the funeral in Texas.

The same year President Johnson found peace, President Nixon found turmoil. Some of his campaign workers had broken into an office of the Democratic National Committee at the Watergate Apartments. It seemed trivial at first, but some people thought President Nixon was lying about knowing anything about the incident.

Ever so slowly over the next year the truth crept out: President Nixon had lied, trying to cover up the petty crime. On August 9, 1974, Richard Nixon became the only president in United States history to resign.

Some critics wanted to tar and feather Billy with President Nixon, saying Billy was an insider. The irony was that Billy had known far more about the inner workings of Lyndon Johnson's White House than Richard Nixon's. But as usual, Billy ignored slander and vicious remarks.

The years of 1973 and 1974 were very hard on the Grahams at home, too. Ruth's father, Nelson Bell, passed away. Ruth's mother died shortly after that. Ruth wobbled on crutches at her mother's funeral, recovering from a severe fall she had taken playing with the grandchildren.

Billy's mother was alive but feeble. Psalm 34 comforted her: "The angel of the LORD encampeth round about them that fear him, and delivereth them." She would live to be nearly ninety. At least the Grahams no longer had to worry about Franklin. He had come to his senses and fully accepted Jesus as his Lord.

BGEA had two major successes in 1975 away from the crusade circuit. Billy's book *Angels* became a best-seller. And World Wide Pictures made its best film ever, *The Hiding Place,* about the heroic ten Boom family of Holland. The family hid Jews and other refugees during World War II at a heavy price: imprisonment in Nazi death camps. In an amazing story of survivalism, spunky, eighty-three-year-old Corrie ten Boom still preached the gospel, living out of a suitcase.

For several years Billy had known Alex Haraszti, a surgeon from Atlanta. Haraszti had emigrated from Hungary to escape Communism. In 1977 Haraszti shocked Billy by asking, "How would you like to hold a full-fledged crusade in Hungary?"

"A crusade for Christ in a Communist country? Of course I would!"

"Leave it to me," said Alex Haraszti.

By late 1977, Billy opened his crusade in a church in Budapest, Hungary. The few hundred Hungarians there were not friendly. Yet, as always, Billy's preaching won their hearts. Their hostility turned into anticipation, then love. By the end of ten days, Billy had preached several times—once to a crowd of thirty thousand!

The Hungarian triumph seemed to break down the barriers to Communist countries. The word spread at the highest levels: Billy was not dangerous. He might even satisfy the people's hunger for God—which never seemed to go away.

The next year, 1978, Billy preached in another Communist country, Poland. Billy always met with Communist officials first. He explained patiently that Christians were good citizens, illustrating with Romans 13 that the Bible instructed Christians to obey authorities. Billy took the officials from the Ten Commandments to Christ's Sermon on the Mount.

Billy began work on the third great goal of his life. The first had been his commitment to preach the gospel of Jesus Christ. The second had been the elimination of racial injustice. The third goal was world peace. And world peace could never be attained without dealing with the Communists.

"To reach the center of Communism, Russia, would be a real triumph for Christ," Billy prayed.

Once again Alex Haraszti helped bring Billy's prayers to reality. Billy arrived in Moscow in May 1982 to preach the gospel of Jesus Christ!

In September 1984, Billy got his first crusade in Russia. If the trip was not triumphant enough for Billy, there was an added victory. Billy's son Franklin, a newly ordained pastor, preached with him.

All that success was dimmed for Billy by a great personal loss. Grady Wilson passed away in 1987. At the funeral, Billy told mourners what a great inspiration Grady had been to him. Billy always regretted how he overshadowed his buddies on the team. Grady had been a fine preacher, and he was the one who loosened up worriers like Lyndon Johnson and Richard Nixon with his barrage of humor.

In America during the 1980s and 1990s, Billy continued citywide crusades, but more and more he preached on an international scale. Beyond America, the Communist world was changing. The Berlin Wall came down.

And Billy achieved another goal: holding a crusade in Communist China. He and Ruth, a "daughter of China," got a rousing welcome in the Great Hall of the People in Beijing. From there Billy began a five-city crusade.

In 1989, BGEA launched Mission World. With communications satellites in space circling the globe, a revival could be beamed to many portable receiving stations all around the world.

From London, Billy spoke live to Britain, Ireland, and ten African countries. Delayed broadcasts were received by another twenty-three African countries. In late 1990, Mission World eventually reached millions in Asia from Billy's live revival in Hong Kong. Some were saying it reached one hundred million viewers!

Communism was unraveling all around the world at an astounding rate. Most shocking of all was the change in Russia. Russians dissolved their Communist government in 1991 and replaced it with a democracy.

In 1992, Billy held a citywide crusade in Moscow. Cliff Barrows could not play the usual music during the altar call. It made the Russians flock to the altar dangerously fast.

"Please walk. Don't run," pleaded Billy. He had never seen such spiritual hunger. The Russians had been denied Christ for seventy-five years!

Over the years Billy had suffered many illnesses: eye problems, kidney stones, hernias, ulcers, tumors, high blood pressure, pneumonia, prostate trouble, and broken ribs. During 1992, his latest affliction was diagnosed: Parkinson's disease. Tiredness and tremors in Billy's hands were the obvious signs of this progressive disorder of the nervous system.

"God comes with greater power when we are weak," answered Billy to anyone who implied he should retire. At seventy-three, Billy not only had nineteen grandchildren, but five great-grandchildren, as well.

In March 1993, from Germany, Billy again preached over a satellite network. This time the team emphasized counseling. BGEA focused not so much on how many people they could reach, but on how many people they could reach where counseling was available.

The new direction called for a new name: Global Mission. In 1995, Global Mission was huge. From Puerto Rico, Billy's sermons went to 30 satellites that sent them on to 3,000 sites in 185 countries around the world. One million counselors were waiting to help the new Christians. The effort did not end there. Tapes were to be shown to more and more sites in the months ahead.

The goal was to reach one billion people!

By 1997, Billy had evangelized in citywide crusades for over fifty years, first in America and then in countries around the world. In moments of exhaustion, Billy thought about retiring.

Only God knew how many people Billy had preached to in one way or another. More than any evangelist in history, he had fulfilled the Great Commission: "Go ye therefore, and teach all nations, baptizing them in the name of the Father, and of the Son, and of the Holy Ghost" (Matthew 28:19).

And yet billions of souls remained to be saved. So Billy, in failing health, would continue to evangelize. As he had said so many times, "I'll keep opening doors. God will sort it all out."

LUIS PALAU

EVANGELIST TO THE WORLD

by W. Terry Whalin

CHAPTER 1

The church bell sounded in the small riverside resort town of Ingeniero-Maschwitz, Argentina, located in the eastern province of Buenos Aires. A crowd gathered in the Catholic church—the only church in town. When the priest called them forward, Luis and Matilde Palau walked to the front. In her arms, Matilde carried their firstborn son.

On November 27, 1934, that son was christened Luis Palau Jr. This tiny baby was beginning a life that would bring thousands of people into a personal relationship with Jesus Christ.

Luis Palau Sr. built a thriving construction business. When Luis Jr. was born, his father was a nonreligious person. His mother attended church, searching for real answers to life's questions. Then the Palaus met Edward Rogers.

As an executive with the Shell Oil Company, Mr. Rogers worked in Argentina. He looked for opportunities to win people to Christ. He and his wife developed a friendship with the Palaus and gave them a copy of the Gospel of Matthew.

Matilde Palau read the book on her knees. When she reached the Beatitudes, she learned that the pure in heart shall see God. She knew her heart wasn't pure. *This is the kind of life I want to live,* she said to herself. *I won't settle for anything less.* Mr. and Mrs. Rogers led Matilde Palau to

Christ, but Mr. Palau didn't want anything to do with what he called "evangelical stuff."

Mrs. Palau began attending the Christian Brethren Church where Mr. Rogers sometimes preached. She asked her husband to go with her, but he refused. Every so often, however, he was seen standing outside the corrugated-metal shed where the Christian Brethren worshiped. He was listening to the sermons.

One day Mr. Palau reluctantly agreed to attend church with his wife and walked into the small chapel. The Palaus sat together, holding one-and-a-half-year-old Luisito, as Luis Jr. was called. Mr. Rogers preached that morning. As Mr. Palau listened to the sermon, he thought about what he had heard over the weeks as he stood in the shadows outside the church. The Holy Spirit convicted him.

Mr. Palau realized the time had come for him to make a decision. And he knew what that decision must be. Without waiting for the sermon to end, he stood up. Using a statement often made by evangelicals in Argentina at that time, he said, "I receive Jesus Christ as my only and sufficient Savior."

Matilde Palau nearly fainted. She was thrilled that her husband would now share her faith, but at the same time she was embarrassed by how he had interrupted the sermon. She hadn't expected her husband to make such a scene.

Almost overnight, Mr. Palau became an active Christian. Few evangelical Christians lived in the town, so the Palaus plunged into Bible study and prayer to learn more about their new faith. Mr. Palau became known for the boldness with which he shared Christ with other people.

As the baby Luis grew up, he watched his parents' activities. Many times he saw his father share his faith and his mother read the Bible. Luis was proud that his parents were committed Christians.

Growing up, Luis spent time with his dad whenever possible. Early in the morning, he often heard his dad open the woodstove to start a fire. Luis would open his eyes and watch his father get the house ready for the day ahead. If he watched long enough, Luis saw his father slip into his office study—a little room along the side of the house. Turning to a chapter in Proverbs, the distinguished man dropped to his knees for prayer and Bible reading.

One day, his father told Luis that each day he read a chapter of Proverbs. There were thirty-one chapters of Proverbs and often thirty-one days in a month. When he grew older, Luis started the same practice—and has continued this pattern he learned from his father throughout his adult life.

Everyone in the Palau family knew about Luis's temper. If something was wrong, or Luis didn't get his way, his temper flared. In a soccer game, the Palau boy gained a reputation for using foul language whenever he felt his team received unfair treatment. Other times at home, Luis would suddenly fly off the handle. He wasn't proud of his anger but didn't know how to handle it.

Early on, Luis attended a government public school. When Luis reached age seven, his father decided to send him to Quilmes Preparatory School. This private British boarding school was located about twenty miles south of Buenos Aires and a little more than forty miles from his home. Lessons were taught in both English and Spanish. World War II, which was destroying Europe and the Pacific, seemed far away.

Luis was one of fifty boarders at the school. Another two hundred boys and girls joined the school for the day classes. Quilmes was excellent preparation for St. Alban's College, which Luis was scheduled to attend when he reached age ten.

Just after his tenth birthday, Luis took his final exams at Quilmes and started to pack for his trip home for the summer (which begins in the middle of December in Argentina). School would be out until the end of summer.

As he worked in his room, Luis got a message that he had a phone call. Hurrying to the phone, he picked up the receiver and heard his grandmother's voice.

"Luis," she said, "your dad is very sick. We really have to pray for him." Although Grandma gave no details, Luis had a terrible feeling.

The next morning, December 17, 1944, Grandma arrived at the school to take Luis to the train station. The three-hour train trip seemed to take forever. Luis could barely stand the suspense and couldn't seem to shake the terrible feelings. Finally, the train arrived in Ingeniero-Maschwitz, and the ten year old anxiously hurried toward home.

Any shred of hope for his father evaporated as Luis got within earshot of his house. He could hear his aunts and uncles moaning and crying.

As Luis ran through the gate, some of his relatives tried to stop him, but he brushed them aside. His father was lying in bed like he was sleeping, but he looked terrible. His skin was yellow and bloated, and his lips were cracked.

Ignoring his four sisters and his other relatives, Luis ran to his father's side and threw his arms around him. But his father's spirit was gone. Luis's mother placed her hands on the young boy's shoulders.

"Luisito, Luisito," she said softly, pulling her son away. "I must talk to you and tell you how it was."

Only ten days earlier, Mr. Palau had gotten sick with bronchial pneumonia. Nothing could be done. Although penicillin was often used to treat pneumonia, it was in short supply. Most medical supplies were being used in Europe and the Pacific to help wounded soldiers involved in the war that had been going on for five years.

Luis's mother said, "We decided to call you so you could hurry home. It was obvious that he was dying, and we gathered around his bed, praying and trying to comfort him. He was struggling to breathe, but suddenly he sat up and began to sing."

Mrs. Palau continued. "Then, when Papito could no longer hold up his head, he fell back on the pillow and said, 'I'm going to be with Jesus, which is far better.'"

Two hours later, at age thirty-five, Luis Palau Sr. had died. His death was in contrast to the typical death scene in the Palaus' town. Often the dying person would cry out in fear of going to hell. Mr. Palau had felt only peace, knowing that he was going to be with Jesus.

As he stood by his father's body, ten-year-old Luis was overwhelmed with grief and anger at everyone and everything. Death was all too real for Luis. One day his father was there, and the next he was gone.

Throughout that summer, Luis peppered his mother with questions about heaven, the second coming of Christ, and the resurrection. Matilde Palau had been a student of the Scriptures for eight years, so she patiently answered her son's questions and dealt with her own grief. Before Luis returned to school, he settled his questions about eternity and heaven. Without any doubt, Luis knew that his father was in heaven with Jesus Christ.

CHAPTER 2

Three months after his father died, Luis prepared to go to St. Alban's College to continue his education. Luis's dreams about education were faced with indifference by many of the people around him, but his mother was determined to follow her husband's wishes.

During the summer break, Mrs. Palau hired someone to manage the family business. She had never been involved in the day-to-day operation of the company. Money had never been a problem in the Palau family, and Luis left for school with the assumption that the family money would never end.

St. Alban's was a tough, all-boys Anglican school. The Argentine government required Spanish education for at least four hours a day, five days a week. Because St. Alban's was a British school, the teachers taught the morning in Spanish and then the rest of the day in English. Different lessons were taught in Spanish than in English. In this bilingual environment, Luis received two years of schooling during each year. When a student completed the four years at St. Alban's, he was prepared for graduate work at Cambridge University. Luis earned pretty good grades, and his days at the school were happy and filled with pranks and practical jokes.

The only dark spot in Luis's life was the news that the manager his mother had hired was not running the business well. For the first time in Luis's life, his family was facing a tight financial situation.

During the days before Luis's summer vacation at the end of 1946, Charles Cohen, a St. Alban's professor, talked with Luis about attending a two-week Christian camp in the mountains along with several dozen other boys. While Luis thought it sounded like fun, he didn't want to give up part of his summer vacation.

Because of his Christian upbringing, Luis could quote Bible verses and sing Christian songs. If pressured, he could even say a prayer. But in his heart, Luis knew he wasn't a Christian.

When Luis discussed going to camp with Mr. Cohen, he protested, saying his family finances were too tight. Then Mr. Cohen offered to pay for the camp. So twelve-year-old Luis agreed. When the school year was over in December, he headed home for several weeks. Camp began in February.

Luis's mother was excited about the idea of her son being at a Christian camp. She told Luis, "I'm not sure you are a real, born-again Christian."

Luis rolled his eyes around saying, "Mom, come on." But his mother knew the truth about her only son.

February finally arrived. Luis had never been to a camp, so he was excited to go to the mountainous area in southern Argentina. It was like the Scouts, with everyone sleeping in Argentine army tents and foldable cots. Fifty or sixty boys from St. Alban's College were there along with Mr. Cohen and several British and American counselors from different missionary organizations.

At the two-week camp, Luis received Bible lessons and memorized Bible verses along with the usual fun and games. There was no contact with the outside world, and Luis missed it. He felt totally cut off from life. He couldn't even learn the soccer scores, and soccer was as big in Argentina as football is in the United States.

At the camp, Mr. Cohen, the normally stiff, curt, and formal teacher, changed into someone completely different. Luis was beginning to like camp, but he knew he couldn't get away from the one tradition at the camp that he dreaded. Each counselor had about ten boys in his tent. One boy was taken each night for a walk and given an opportunity to say yes or no to Christ's claims on his life.

Every night, Luis waited with a sick feeling in the pit of his stomach to be told that it was his turn to walk with Frank Chandler, his counselor. Every night, some other boy's name was called. Finally, every other boy in his tent had walked with Frank. Luis knew that this night would be his turn.

Even though Luis felt guilty for his sins, he didn't want to face the issue of his salvation. *Maybe I'll pretend to be asleep and Frank will go away,* Luis thought. The counselor came and shook Luis, but the boy continued pretending to be asleep. Finally, Frank dumped Luis on the ground.

"Come on, Luis," Frank said. "Get up." The pair walked

outside the tent and sat down on a fallen tree. A light rain was beginning to fall.

"Luis," Frank said, "are you a born-again Christian?"

"I don't think so," Luis said.

"It's not a matter of whether you think so or not. Are you or aren't you?" Frank persisted.

"No, I'm not," Luis said slowly.

"If you died tonight," Frank asked Luis, "would you go to heaven or hell?"

For a moment, Luis sat quietly and thought about his answer. "I'm going to hell."

"Is that where you want to go?"

"No," Luis said.

"Then why are you going there?" Frank asked.

With a shrug of his shoulders, Luis said, "I don't know."

Frank flipped open the pages of his Bible and read from the apostle Paul's letter to the Romans using Luis's name: "If you confess with your lips [Luis] that Jesus is Lord and believe in your heart that God raised him from the dead, you [Luis] will be saved. For man believes with his heart and so is justified, and he confesses with his lips and so is saved" (Romans 10:9–10, RSV).

After reading, Frank looked up and said, "Luis, do you believe in your heart that God raised Jesus from the dead?"

"Yes, I do," Luis said.

"Then what do you have to do next to be saved?"

As it began to rain even harder, Luis hesitated. Frank

reread verse 9: " 'If you confess with your lips that Jesus is Lord. . .you will be saved.' "

"Luis, are you ready to confess Jesus as your Lord now?"

"Yes."

"All right, let's pray." Frank put his arm around Luis's shoulders and led him in a prayer.

Luis prayed, "Lord Jesus, I believe You were raised from the dead. I confess You with my lips. Give me eternal life. I want to be Yours. Save me from hell. Amen."

After the prayer, Luis began to cry. He gave Frank a big hug then they ran back to the tent. When Luis crawled under his blanket, he pulled out his flashlight and wrote two lines in his Bible: "February 12, 1947" and "I received Jesus Christ."

At age twelve, Luis Palau knew he was a member of God's family. "When compared to eternal life with Christ, every other decision seems unimportant," Luis said later.

When Luis returned home and told his mother, she was ecstatic. The excitement about his decision lasted for several months. While not obnoxious about his faith, Luis began to carry his Bible often and became more active in the Crusaders youth group at school.

Because of the time he spent with Mr. Cohen at camp, Luis felt close to his teacher. He pitched in to help with the Crusaders youth group meetings held in the Cohen home Sunday afternoons. Some of his friends at school didn't know how to accept Luis's increased Christian activity.

As time passed, Luis started to have less excitement

about Christ. He wasn't sure what the reason was. Maybe it was the constant pressure from his friends at school to listen to soccer matches and attend movies. Whatever the reason, while he continued to be active in Christian activities, Luis's initial excitement about the gospel began to dim.

One day when Luis returned to school from a Crusaders meeting, he carelessly left his Bible on a streetcar and lost it. Without a copy of the Bible, Luis quickly lost his enthusiasm over Bible classes and almost anything else concerning his commitment to Christ.

One day Luis was showing off in art class. Mr. Thompson, the new art teacher, walked over and made a sarcastic remark about Luis's horrible painting of a tree. Luis knew the painting was bad. As the teacher turned and walked away, Luis spat out a foul word in Spanish. Since Mr. Thompson had recently come from England, Luis figured the teacher wouldn't know the word. But the other students understood and roared with laughter.

"What did you say, Palau?" the teacher asked.

"Oh, nothing, Mr. Thompson, Sir. Nothing, really."

"No, what was it, Palau?"

"It was really nothing important, Sir."

"I'd really like to hear it again, Palau. Would you mind repeating it?"

"Oh, I don't think it's worth repeating. I—"

"All right," Mr. Thompson snapped. "Go see the master on duty."

The class was stunned. At St. Alban's, to see the master on duty was the ultimate form of punishment. The fearful role of disciplinarian rotated among the professors. No one tells the master on duty why the student has come for punishment. The student must tell the master himself, then take whatever punishment is given. Luis cringed when he saw that Mr. Cohen was the master on duty.

"Come in, Palau," Mr. Cohen said. "Why are you here?"

"Mr. Thompson sent me."

"Is that so? Why?"

For someone whom Luis had spent a lot of time with in Crusaders meetings and summer camp, Mr. Cohen acted terribly cold and distant.

"Well, I said a bad word," Luis confessed.

"Repeat it," Mr. Cohen directed.

"Oh, I had better not," Luis said.

"Repeat it," the teacher insisted.

Luis hung his head and repeated the word from art class. The teacher sat and stared in disappointment at Luis. Then he reached around for his cricket bat.

"You know, Palau, I'm going to give you six of the best," he said. It was the maximum amount of punishment.

"Bend and touch your toes, please," Mr. Cohen said. "Before I punish you, I want to tell you this, Palau. You are the greatest hypocrite I have ever seen in my life."

Luis winced at the strong words.

"You think you get away with your arrogant, cynical,

above-it-all, know-it-all attitude, but I have watched you. You come to Bible class, all right, but you are a hypocrite."

The physical punishment stung for days. It hurt horribly whenever Luis had to sit down. He slept on his stomach for a week. For the next several months, Luis hated Mr. Cohen. He quit attending the Crusaders meetings and didn't pay any attention during Bible classes. At church services, Luis walked through the motions but tuned out any teaching.

Luis's relationship with God was broken. Luis turned to school dances and reading magazines about car racing and sports on Sunday. He quickly became a fast-talking, smooth-working phony. He chose non-Christian kids for friends. They did what Luis had been taught were sins—going to soccer games on Sundays, wasting time, and fantasizing about girls. He never talked with these friends about Christ or what the Lord could do for their lives. Instead, Luis went along with the crowd and their activities—until Carnival Week.

CHAPTER 3

In many South American countries, the week before Lent is marked with wild abandonment. In Argentina, it's called Carnival Week. Most businesses close for the entire week, and just about any kind of behavior is allowed.

Luis had grown tired of the little parties and games from past years. He decided that if he got involved in Carnival Week events, he could firmly cut his ties with Christianity.

Luis's friends planned to pick him up for the first day of the weeklong celebration. He knew many of the activities were wrong, so the night before, he fell to his knees beside his bed and pleaded with God, "Get me out of this, and I will give up everything that's of the world. I will serve You and give my whole life to You. Just get me out of this!"

Sometimes God answers prayer in amazing ways! The next morning Luis slowly sat up and noticed his mouth felt strange. Stumbling to a mirror, Luis saw that he looked like he had swallowed a Ping-Pong ball. Then Luis managed a crooked smile in the mirror. Out loud he said, "God has answered my prayer!"

On the telephone, Luis reached one of his friends, "I can't go to the dance tonight, and I won't be going to the carnival all this week."

"Come on, Luis!" the friend protested. "Everything has been planned!"

"No," Luis said. "I have a good reason, and I will not go."

"I'm coming over," he insisted. "You must be crazy."

A few minutes later, the young man arrived with three or four other friends, but Luis had made up his mind not to attend Carnival Week. His friends left, admitting defeat. Firm in his decision, Luis walked inside, determined to destroy the things that kept him from following Jesus. He tore up his university club membership card and ripped up his soccer and car-racing magazines. He also tossed out many record albums.

The next day, Luis went to church morning and night. While the rest of his town was caught up in the merrymaking of Carnival Week, Luis returned to the Lord.

Having repaired his relationship with God, Luis needed to decide what to do with the rest of his life. Since he was finished with school, he decided it was time to begin a career. Although he was only in his midteens, Luis lived in a time and place where boys were expected to take on serious responsibilities at a young age.

Because Luis had a bilingual British education, the Bank of London hired him as a junior employee-in-training. Luis gained a reputation as a go-getter. In a short time, Luis received several promotions, mostly because he was bilingual.

One day Luis submitted some papers, asking for a transfer to Cordoba so he could live closer to his mother and sisters. He was taking a much bigger risk than it might seem. No one ever asked for a transfer in the bank where Luis worked. To do so was to risk being fired or laughed out of the office. But Luis felt it was important to be nearer his family. Trusting that God would work out the situation for the best, Luis kept on working and waited for a response.

One day, Luis received a memo asking him to report to the personnel office. Full of fear, he walked to the office.

"Why do you want to transfer to Cordoba?" the personnel manager asked Luis.

"My mother and sisters live there. In addition, I know the bank has a good branch in the city," Luis said.

An uncomfortable silence filled the room.

"You know," the manager said, "it would be good for you. In a branch of that size, you can learn banking more quickly since only one or two people are in each major department. In fact, we'll put this down as if it were our idea. Then we can justify paying for your move and giving you a promotion and raise."

Luis felt stunned. The manager continued, "If you progress as nicely there as you have here at headquarters, within six months we'll put you in charge of foreign operations of that branch, and in a year we'll bring you back here for a few weeks of specialized training. In our eyes, you will begin as the number four man in Cordoba." Luis hadn't reached his eighteenth birthday.

Time passed quickly as Luis's move was approved, and he gathered his belongings. His sisters and mother were excited to learn that he would once again be near home.

A few weeks before his move to Cordoba, Luis was lying

on the living room floor at his uncle Arnold and aunt Marjorie's home. Luis tuned in a shortwave radio program from HCJB in Quito, Ecuador. He didn't catch the preacher's name, but Luis heard him calling men to come to Jesus Christ. Later, he realized that he had been listening to Billy Graham. On that living room floor, Luis prayed, "Jesus, someday use me on the radio to bring others to You, just as this program has firmed up my resolve to completely live for You."

Soon Luis was settled in Cordoba. He became involved in a church, and when he was eighteen years old, he taught a Sunday school class of young boys. One of the members of his class faced a family crisis—his parents were separated. Divorce wasn't common in Argentina at that time, and any sign of marriage problems was frowned on. The boy was having a hard time adjusting to his family situation and the unkind comments people made.

The boy listened intently when Luis taught the class, but he never spoke. Later that week, Luis visited the boy at his grandmother's house and led him into a personal relationship with Christ.

The next week, the boy wasn't in class, so Luis went to see his grandmother. She told him the story. After accepting Christ, the boy was riding his bike and grabbed hold of a streetcar. The bike slipped under the wheels of the streetcar and the youngster was killed instantly.

The grandmother told Luis, "My grandson is in heaven now, and we are at peace." Luis learned to speak for Christ whenever God opened the door of opportunity.

Throughout this time of his life, Luis had one central thought: Take care of your family. Over the years, his mother's financial situation had gotten worse. Luis lived with his four sisters and mother in a small house. Even with his job, there wasn't enough money to provide for six adults. Some nights, the family supper amounted to a loaf of French bread with some garlic flavoring. The family never complained about the slim meals. Often during the brief meal, Mrs. Palau read from a devotional book such as Charles Spurgeon's *Checkbook of Faith*.

At the bank, Luis's coworkers began to call him "Pastor." He used his free time at work for Bible study. He still dreamed of being an evangelist. While Luis studied, prayed, taught, and witnessed, he saw few results from his efforts.

Luis read the stories of great evangelists and was excited about how they were used by God in people's lives. Yet it seemed obvious to Luis that he didn't have whatever the gift was that they had. Finally Luis gave God a deadline. *If I don't see any converts by the end of this year, Lord, then I'll quit preaching,* Luis prayed. The end of the year arrived without any changes. Luis decided God must have something different for him to do.

About four days into the new year, Luis purchased a Spanish version of Billy Graham's *The Secret of Happiness*. He curled up on the couch to study the book. Despite his low feelings about his evangelism and service to God, Luis was encouraged by Billy Graham's thoughts about the Beatitudes from the Sermon on the Mount in Matthew 5. While reading, he memorized the major points for each beatitude.

That evening, Luis thought about skipping the home Bible study, but out of loyalty to the elders, he caught the bus to the meeting. After several hymns, the speaker still hadn't arrived. The host said, "Luis, you're going to have to speak. None of the other preachers are here."

Luis protested, "I'm not prepared, and besides I didn't bring my Bible."

The host wouldn't be deterred. "Look, Luis, there's no one else. You have to speak."

With hardly time to breathe a prayer, Luis borrowed a New Testament and turned to Matthew 5. He read a beatitude, then repeated a few points from Billy Graham's book. After several verses, he reached the beatitude, "Blessed are the pure in heart, for they shall see God" (Matthew 5:8, RSV).

Suddenly a woman stood and began to cry, "Somebody help me! My heart is not pure. How am I going to find God?"

Luis told the people to turn to 1 John 1:7 where they read, "The blood of Jesus his Son cleanses us from all sin" (RSV). He explained God's plan of salvation, and the woman discovered peace with God.

That evening, Luis learned some important lessons. It wasn't his job to convict people of sin. The Holy Spirit did that. Luis was the vehicle God used to lead the repentant woman to Christ. Perhaps Luis could be an evangelist after all.

Luis began to dream about mass evangelism where hundreds and thousands of people could be won to Christ. As Luis prayed and read about mass evangelism, he became certain of one thing: He didn't want to be involved in such crusades if his purpose was to get a great reputation. From the beginning, Luis sensed that if his ego got out of hand, the Lord would quickly put him in his place. So he simply prayed, "Lord, please make everything I do pleasing to You." Luis shifted his personal study into high gear.

One day in late 1958, Luis received a flier announcing a meeting with two Americans: Dick Hillis, a former missionary to China, and Ray Stedman, a pastor from Palo Alto, California. At the meeting, speaking English, Luis introduced himself to Pastor Stedman.

Pastor Stedman asked Luis many questions and was genuinely interested in the answers. Luis was flattered when Pastor Stedman invited him to a Bible study with a few missionaries the next morning.

After the Bible study, Pastor Stedman needed to shop in town, so Luis gave him a ride on his motorbike. "Would you like to go to seminary?" Pastor Stedman asked.

"It would be nice, but I'm not sure I'll ever make it," Luis answered. "I don't have a lot of money, and my church doesn't encourage formal theological education."

"Well," Pastor Stedman said, "it could be arranged if the Lord wanted it. How would you like to come to the United States?"

"I've thought about it," Luis admitted. "Maybe someday I'll be able to go, the Lord willing." He thought the conversation was simply about dreams.

"You know, Luis," Stedman said, "the Lord may just will it."

The next night, Luis took Dick Hillis and Ray Stedman to the airport. "I'll see you in the United States," Pastor Stedman promised.

"Well, the Lord willing, maybe someday," Luis said.

"No, Luis, the Lord is going to will. I'll write you from the plane."

As Luis left the airport, he thought about Ray Stedman. The man seemed warm and flattering, yet a bit unrealistic. Why bother to dream?

A few days later, Ray's letter arrived with the news that he knew a businessman who wanted to finance Luis's trip to the United States so that Luis could study at Dallas Theological Seminary. At first, Luis found the news thrilling, but then he changed his mind because so many people in Argentina needed the good news about Jesus. He didn't want to spend four years in seminary, and who would take care of his family? He wrote Stedman and declined his offer.

Immediately, Stedman wrote again, assuring Luis that someone from the United States would also provide for the needs of his family. The opportunity seemed too incredible, so Luis put off answering for several months. Although Luis knew it was rude not to answer, he ignored a couple more letters.

Things were also changing at the bank. One day Luis confronted the bank manager about some new policies. Because of his Christian testimony, Luis told the manager that he couldn't meet the requirements for his job with a clear conscience. The practices weren't illegal, but they raised ethical questions. The manager reminded Luis about how much the bank had done for him and what they planned for his future. Luis didn't back down. After that conversation, he could feel a change in atmosphere at the bank.

One day at work, Luis met Keith Bentson, who worked at SEPAL, the Latin American division of a company named OC International. Keith was looking for a Christian to translate English material into Spanish. Luis jumped at the opportunity to change jobs—even though it meant a cut in his pay.

While at SEPAL, Luis continued holding evangelistic tent meetings throughout the city of Cordoba. He dreamed of pulling together a team of people to conduct crusades but had no idea how that would happen because his money was too tight to hire anyone.

One night after a meeting, an American, Bruce Woodman, introduced himself to Luis and asked if he wanted a soloist or a song leader for his meetings. Luis instantly agreed to add Bruce to the team, as well as Bill Fasig, who could play either the organ or piano for meetings. A team was born.

CHAPTER 4

The excitement of evangelistic meetings and working for SEPAL gave Luis one more excuse for not answering Ray Stedman's letters. Pastor Stedman continued to invite Luis to go to the United States and get additional training. His unanswered letters grew more urgent, yet Luis didn't respond to them.

Finally, Pastor Stedman wrote a stinging letter that said the inaction from Luis was rude and irresponsible. In spite of Luis's failure to respond to his letters, Stedman made it clear that if he wanted, Luis could still come to the United States. Stedman encouraged Luis to study at Dallas Theological Seminary but also said Luis wouldn't be forced to study there or anywhere else for four years.

"Too many people are going to hell for me to be spending four more years reading books," Luis wrote in a letter to Pastor Stedman. "I can study at home. I'm disciplined, and I enjoy studying. What I need is an opportunity to ask questions of some good Bible teachers and get answers to the really tough ones I haven't been able to resolve through my own reading."

Ray Stedman told Luis about a one-year graduate course in theology at Multnomah Biblical Seminary in Portland, Oregon. He also offered an internship for Luis in his

California church before and after the school year. Then Pastor Stedman sent money for Luis's mother to reassure him that support would continue while Luis was in the United States. Pastor Stedman also enclosed a check so Luis could travel to Buenos Aires and get his passport. Every excuse was covered. For a long time, Luis had wanted to go to the United States. So he prayed about going and agreed to go to California.

A small crowd of family and friends gathered with Luis Palau at the Ezeiza International Airport in Buenos Aires. Luis was traveling to the United States on the first airline flight of his life. During the tearful farewell, his mother just couldn't get in enough last-minute advice.

She said, "Don't go into the cities; don't travel alone; watch out; don't get shot and stuffed into a trunk, and remember Hebrews 13:5 and 6!" She was worried about murder, but Luis was worried about the trip. The pair hugged in the airport, and Luis turned to go. Luis was wearing his only brand-new, black suit.

The old DC-6 chugged over the Andes Mountains, then settled into a lower altitude to take the strain off the engines. Every time the plane climbed or suddenly dropped in altitude, Luis had a stomachache. Luis stared out the window, and said in his best English, "Look at all those little white boats."

His seat mate rose and leaned across to look. "Those are clouds, kid," he said in a bored tone of voice.

The flight reached Miami ten hours late, so Luis missed

his connecting flight. He was exhausted. His new suit looked rumpled, and Luis was worried. Three thousand miles away, Ray Stedman was expecting him to speak in his church.

After a collect call to Pastor Stedman and a sorry attempt at a few hours of sleep, Luis was on a Delta jet headed to San Francisco. Luis could not believe the airline. Delta gave away many free cups of coffee, sugar, plastic spoons, maps, and postcards. *This must be the land of opportunity,* Luis thought.

As the jet moved across the nation, it stopped in cities like Atlanta. *Someday we'll have evangelistic crusades here,* Luis thought. It was only a dream. Luis had never seen a crusade, let alone preached at one, but in his heart, he felt a burden from God. It was only a matter of time. The first step would take place in California. The plane landed, and Luis began a new life.

"Luis, stay with me everywhere I go," Ray Stedman said as Luis began his internship at Palo Alto Bible Church. "It's the best way for you to learn."

The pastor's calendar was full of counseling appointments. Through every session, Luis sat in the corner behind the counselee. "Don't worry about Luis," Pastor Stedman told the counselee. "He's just learning." Soon the person forgot about Palau sitting in the corner of the room. Luis watched the pastor work with people.

One day, Bob, a member of the church, asked for an appointment. Luis dreaded sitting through that meeting because Bob consistently caused trouble for Pastor Stedman.

What will happen during this session? Luis wondered.

"I'm here to give you some money for the church," Bob began, pulling out a check for fifteen thousand dollars and giving it to the pastor. The Palo Alto Bible Church was booming and could certainly use the unexpected gift.

As Luis watched, Pastor Stedman walked over to Bob, picked up the check, and tore it into small pieces. "I don't care about your money, Bob," the pastor said. "I care about your soul. You're not going to buy my affection. You need to give your life to Jesus Christ."

After Bob walked out of the room, Luis asked Pastor Stedman, "How are you able to go so fast and decide so quickly what is the heart of the issue?"

"Never speak to the mask," Ray Stedman explained. "Everyone wears a mask about his or her true problem, but you need to get behind the mask."

Pastor Stedman cut through false piety and emphasized a commitment to the Bible for every action. It was an important lesson that would help Luis with his counseling in the years ahead.

Two months with the Stedman family was hardly enough time for Luis to plunge into American culture. He needed to learn how to eat and behave like other people in the country. But it was all the time he had before traveling north to Multnomah Biblical Seminary in Portland, Oregon.

In his first term at Multnomah, Luis found his studies were a challenge. While he had done a lot of reading and studying, Luis knew little about some of the more technical areas of study he now faced. Sometimes Luis felt frustrated not to be able to live with joy, release, and freedom like Ray Stedman and several other Christians he had met. The more Luis desired a deeper life with Christ, the more it seemed to elude him.

The other students and faculty at Multnomah treated Luis royally. To them, Luis looked like a friendly, winsome, and somewhat different South American. Unknown to them, Luis faced discouragement and spiritual battles. If Luis hadn't cared so much about his service to Christ and preaching the gospel, he might have given up during the first term and gone back to Argentina.

Luis reached a new low around Thanksgiving. The second term would start in only a month. Luis felt it was a hopeless dream to be able to attend. A friend at Ray Stedman's church had paid for his first term, but Luis had no money for the rest of the year. *As soon as the term is over, I'm going back to Argentina,* Luis decided.

That weekend, Luis checked his mailbox for a letter from home. The only thing in the box was a plain envelope with his name on it. The teachers used the mailboxes for returning graded papers, so Luis assumed another assignment was in the envelope. When he pulled the paper out, Luis saw a simple typewritten letter without any identification or signature. It read:

Dear Luis,

You have been a great blessing to many of us here in the States, and we appreciate what you have taught us. We feel that you deserve help to finish your year at Multnomah; therefore, all your tuition and books have been paid for.

Just check in at the business office, and they will finalize the papers. So you will be grateful to every American you have met or will ever meet, we remain anonymous.

So God is still with me after all! Luis thought.

During that year, Luis developed a growing interest in a member of his class—Patricia Scofield. One evening, Luis and several others went to a class party. Luis asked Pat, "May I walk you over?"

She said, "Sure." It was no big deal, and they weren't even together at the party. But Luis became interested. To Luis, Pat seemed mature and smart—and she knew how to dress well. As they talked, Luis learned that Pat was spiritually sensitive. As he walked across the campus to his classes, Luis began to keep an eye out for Pat.

CHAPTER 5

Luis grew more and more discouraged about his spiritual life. He was taking a course called Spiritual Life, taught by Dr. George Kehoe. Dr. Kehoe began each class by quoting Galatians 2:20: "I have been crucified with Christ; it is no longer I who live, but Christ who lives in me; and the life I now live in the flesh I live by faith in the Son of God, who loved me and gave himself for me." (RSV)."

The verse was a gnawing reminder to Luis of the lack of fruit in his spiritual life. He was frustrated at his failure. If asked to describe himself, Luis would have said that he was envious, jealous, preoccupied, self-centered, and overly ambitious.

Shortly before Christmas break, Major Ian Thomas spoke at the Multnomah chapel service. Luis had begun sitting in the back of the auditorium during chapel services. Usually the chapel services were another dose of exposition or missionary stories. In the back of the room, he dared the speaker to make him pay attention. If the speaker was good, he then honored him by listening. Otherwise, Luis daydreamed or peeked at his class notes.

Major Thomas was founder and general director of the Torchbearers, the group that runs the Capernwray Hall Bible School in England. His British accent and staccato delivery were unusual, but what really intrigued Luis was the way Thomas pointed with a partially amputated finger. Thomas's twenty-two-minute message brought some dramatic changes for Palau.

Ian Thomas talked about Moses spending forty years in the wilderness to learn that he was nothing. Then one day, Moses was confronted with a burning bush. Thomas said that the burning bush was likely a dry bunch of ugly little sticks that had hardly developed, yet Moses had to take off his shoes. Why? Because this was holy ground. God was in the bush! God was telling Moses, "I don't need a pretty bush or an educated bush or an eloquent bush. Any old bush will do, as long as I am in the bush. If I am going to use you, I am going to use you. It will not be you doing something for Me, but Me doing something through you."

The illustration hit Luis in a fresh way. He was that type of bush: a worthless, useless bunch of dried-up sticks. Palau could do nothing for God. All of his reading, studying, asking questions, and trying to model himself after others was worthless—unless God was in the bush. And only God could make something happen.

To close his message, Thomas read Galatians 2:20. All at once, Luis understood the passage. " 'I have been crucified with Christ; it is no longer I who live, but Christ who lives in me (RSV).' " His biggest spiritual struggle was finally over! He decided to let God be God and then let Luis Palau depend on Him.

A tremendous spiritual release flooded Luis. He ran back to his room, and in tears, fell to his knees next to his bunk. He prayed in Spanish, "Lord, now I understand! The whole thing is 'not I, but Christ in me.' It's not what I'm going to do for You but rather what You are going to do through me."

For the next hour and a half, Luis stayed on his knees and continued praying. He asked God to forgive his pride. *Oh, I was really something, but God was not active in the bush. I hadn't given Him a chance.* Luis allowed God to take control of his life.

That day marked a turning point in Luis's spiritual life. The practical working out of that discovery would be lengthy and painful, but at last the realization had come. Luis could begin to relax and rest in Jesus.

In the meantime, Luis began to get better acquainted with Pat Scofield outside of class. By Valentine's Day, they were unofficially engaged. A quick meeting with the college president allowed them to make it official a few days later.

Not long after that, Pat noticed that Luis seemed to be a bit reluctant to talk about their upcoming marriage. "Luis, my dad has been figuring out how to get enough money to pay for our wedding," Pat said.

"Pay for the wedding?" Luis repeated. "What does that mean?"

"It's the custom that the parents of the bride pay for the wedding," Pat explained.

"Everything?" Luis asked, his tone rising in excitement.

"Of course—except for possibly the rehearsal dinner, and we can go simple on that," Pat added.

Relief passed across Luis's face. "Then what are we waiting for?"

Luis had known his finances were incredibly tight. His mother and sisters couldn't afford to pay for anything to do with the wedding. In Argentina, the couples split the expenses fifty-fifty. Luis was glad to learn the custom was different in America!

At the end of the school year, Luis headed back to Palo Alto to continue his internship with Ray Stedman, while Pat stayed in Portland. For two long months, the couple wrote letters. They had no money for phone calls. In one of these letters, Luis wrote Pat about a conversation with one of the elders, Bob Connell.

Throughout his internship, Luis had not told anyone about the secret dreams of his heart—evangelism and evangelistic crusades.

One day Bob had pulled Luis aside and said, "Luis, I believe God is going to use you to win as many souls as Billy Graham—even in this country." Luis didn't know what to say in response.

After completing his internship, Luis raced back up the coast in an old '55 Buick he had bought from Ray Stedman. He arrived in Portland just a few days before the wedding. On August 5, 1961, Pastor Wollen and Ray Stedman officiated at Luis and Pat's marriage.

After a two-week honeymoon, the Palaus drove back to the San Francisco Bay area. After they were interviewed by the OC International board, the Palaus were accepted for missionary service. Then they drove back to Portland and packed for their missionary internship in Detroit.

"America the free." The words meant something to Luis. From his first days in the U.S., he loved the freedom to travel and the cleanliness and order of the society. But each January, Luis had to register again with the U.S. government. He constantly lived with the fear that if he made a mistake of any kind, he would be shipped back to Argentina on the first Pan American flight out of the country.

After his marriage to Pat, Luis applied to become an American citizen. It was not a simple process. He had to learn the Preamble to the United States Constitution, the Pledge of Allegiance, and take an examination. Then he appeared in front of a United States judge and renounced any allegiance to Argentina and his citizenship in that country. He was embracing America and found the experience invigorating—almost like a conversion.

Immediately after the ceremony, Luis climbed into his old Buick and drove to a bridge along the Old Bayshore Freeway. He parked his car and leaned over the bridge. In his hand, Luis had his old green card. The document gave him permission to live and work in the United States even though he wasn't a citizen. He no longer needed it. *Rip!* Luis tore it into tiny pieces and tossed it off the bridge. As the green pieces of paper fluttered down into the bay, he shouted, "I'm an American! Nobody can kick me out of this country!"

Besides becoming an American, Luis reached another milestone that summer of 1962—Pat discovered she was pregnant. Luis was going to be a father.

CHAPTER 6

In January 1963, Pat was seven months pregnant. While doing missionary fund-raising work at Valley Church in Cupertino, California, the Palaus were staying in the home of some friends. Pat suddenly announced it was time to go to the hospital. Luis couldn't believe it. He reminded Pat about their plan for their first child—to return home to Portland in two months. The baby couldn't come now.

"Tell that to the baby," Pat said.

They headed to Stanford University Hospital. After Luis had been waiting for more than an hour in the hallway, the doctor, a Christian friend from Palo Alto, came and said there were serious complications. Luis paced the hallway, and, after several hours, assumed the baby had been lost, or the doctor would have returned. Then the doctor walked down the hall with a huge grin.

"Congratulations!" he said. "You're the father of twin boys!" Kevin and Keith were premature and weighed less than four pounds each. They stayed in the hospital for five weeks before they were finally brought home.

The rest of the year was busy as the Palaus adjusted to having doubled their family's size. Later that year, Luis was ordained at Ray Stedman's church. Then the Palaus flew to Costa Rica, where they were going to attend language school. It was Pat's first time outside of the U.S. The twins weren't quite a year old. Pat cried because of the overwhelming adjustments, but several students who attended the language school with the Palaus created a fun Christmas that year to help ease the cultural shock.

During the summer of 1964, the Palaus arrived in Bogota, Colombia. As new missionaries, their assignment was training men and women in evangelism and church planting. Luis and several others held Colombia's first evangelistic street meetings after a decade of violent persecutions and killings. The Palaus and others felt change was in the air for Colombia.

Later that year, Luis and several others flew back to Quito, Ecuador. They were going to launch a new evangelistic concept on television. At HCJB, Luis opened the telephone lines for live counseling television broadcasts with the potential to reach large numbers of people for Christ.

Initially, they started with a short program, but long after it went off the air, people continued to call the station. After a couple weeks, they were on the air for three hours at a time. Luis found the experience both invigorating and exhausting. The Lord had given him the ability to think quickly under pressure, but the program required rapid recall of specific passages from the Bible. Luis was forced to study the Bible with renewed vengeance. He had to store up God's answers for difficult problems in life.

Once the program went on the air, Luis never knew what

to expect. One person would call who was on the verge of suicide; the next caller would be going through a messy divorce.

One night, Luis received two phone calls in a row. The first conversation was one of the most rewarding he had while working on the program, and the second turned into one of the most bizarre encounters of his ministry.

The first caller was a young flight attendant. She had sinned deeply and felt miserable, repentant, and desperate to be forgiven.

Until that evening, Luis had not led callers to Christ on the air. Instead, he counseled them from the Scriptures and set up an in-person appointment the next day. In the studio counseling office, he could carefully show them the way of salvation. But when this desperate caller heard Luis read from the Bible about God's offer of forgiveness and salvation, she wanted to receive Christ immediately. He hesitated and thought, *Would it look like a setup? This woman is obviously sincere about her decision.*

Luis asked her to pray with him, then added that anyone else watching by television who wanted to pray along with them and receive Christ could do so. "Dear God," he began, "I know I am a sinner." She repeated each line.

Luis and the woman prayed on and recounted what she had already explained through the phone call. "Father, I need Your forgiveness and Your saving love." As she prayed to receive Christ, Luis experienced a tearful, solemn moment. The young woman who trusted Christ on the air insisted on an appointment the next morning at 9:00.

The next caller was brief. A tiny, high-pitched, squeaky voice simply asked for an appointment the next day at 9:30. There was no more conversation. When Luis agreed to the time, the squeaky voice simply thanked him and hung up.

The next morning, Luis encouraged the young flight attendant in her newfound faith. As he walked her to the door and gave her a Bible and some literature, Luis noticed a little woman walking through the gates of the HCJB property. Two huge, able-bodied men walked close behind the woman. When she entered the office, Luis asked if the two gentlemen would like to come inside, as well.

"No," she said, "one will stand by the door and the other by the gate." The person with the squeaky voice from the night before had arrived right on schedule. When she entered the room, she brushed past Luis and began to feel along the edges of the desk top as though she was searching for something. With no explanation, she moved to the wall and checked behind a hanging picture, then her eyes traveled to every corner of the room before she sat down.

She must be unbalanced, Luis thought.

As they talked, Luis became convinced the woman was unlike anyone he had ever met. She attacked each cigarette she took from her purse, sucking every last bit from it and lighting the next with the smoldering butt of the last one.

"You pastors and priests," she began with disgust. "You are a bunch of thieves and liars and crooks. All you want is to deceive people; all you want is money!" For more than twenty minutes, she continued with this type of talk. She swore constantly and accused and criticized. So much bitterness gushed from her that it left Luis speechless.

"Madam," Luis finally said, "is there anything I can do for you? How can I help you?"

She slowly took her cigarette from her lips and sat staring at Luis for an instant. Suddenly, she broke into uncontrollable sobs. After several minutes, Luis noticed the edge had disappeared from her voice. "You know," she said, "in the thirty-eight years I have lived, you are the first person who has ever asked me if he could help me."

"What is your name?" Luis asked.

Suddenly her tone changed, and she looked hard again. "Why do you want to know my name?"

"Well, you've said a lot of things here, and I don't even know how to address you. I just want to know how to address you."

She shifted in her chair and sat straighter. "I'm going to tell you," she announced, as if allowing Luis to know her name was giving him a privilege. "My name is Maria Benitez-Perez," she said triumphantly.

Luis recognized her last name as that of a large family of wealth and influence. "I am the secretary of the Communist Party here in Ecuador. I am a Marxist-Leninist, and I am a materialist. I don't believe in God."

For the next three hours, without pause or interruption,

Maria talked. As a Marxist-Leninist, she made it quite clear that she opposed everything about Christianity. Luis continued listening and praying, *When will the opening come?*

"Listen, Palau," Maria finally said. "Supposing there is a God—and I'm not saying there is, because I don't believe the Bible, and I don't believe there's a God—but just supposing there is. Just for the sake of chatting about it, if there is a God—which there isn't—do you think He would receive a woman like me?"

So this little woman with the bold attitude had a chink in her armor after all! Years before, Luis had studied Dr. R. A. Torrey's book, *How to Work for Christ.* He learned that when dealing with a professed atheist, the best approach is to take one verse from the Bible and stay with it, driving it home until it sticks, repeating it as many times as necessary. The Bible says that the law of the Lord converts the soul, Dr. Torrey wrote, not the arguments of men.

Which verse suits her? Luis wondered. As he prayed, the Lord reminded him of Hebrews 10:17, one of Luis's favorite verses: "I will remember their sins and their misdeeds no more" (RSV).

Luis said, "Look, Maria, don't worry about what I think; look at what God thinks." He opened his Bible to the verse and let Maria read it.

"But I don't believe the Bi—"

"You've already told me that," Luis interrupted. "But we're just supposing there's a God, right? Let's just suppose this is His Word. He says, 'Their sins and their lawless deeds I will remember no more.' "

She waited, as if she was expecting Luis to say more. He sat there in silence as she recounted a list of her sins.

Luis said, " 'I will remember their sins and their misdeeds no more.' " Internally, he began to count the times he repeated it.

"But I haven't told you half of my story. I stabbed a comrade who later committed suicide."

" 'I will remember their sins and their misdeeds no more.' "

"I've led student riots where people were killed!"

" 'I will remember their sins and their misdeeds no more.' "

"I egged on my friends and then hid while they were out dying for our cause."

" 'I will remember their sins and their misdeeds no more.' "

Seventeen times Luis responded to Maria's objections and confessions with that one Bible verse. It was past lunchtime. He felt tired and weak. "Would you like Christ to forgive all that you've told me about, and all the rest I don't even know?"

She was silent. Finally, she spoke softly and said, "If He could forgive me and change me, it would be the greatest miracle in the world." Luis led her in a simple prayer of commitment. By the end, she was crying.

A week later, Maria came back to HCJB and told Luis she was reading the Bible and felt a lot better. A longtime missionary from HCJB agreed to follow up on Maria, and Luis didn't see her again for two months.

In January 1966, a month before the Palaus' third son, Andrew, was born, Luis returned to Quito for more television counseling and radio program taping. While in Ecuador, Luis visited Maria and was shocked at her appearance because her face was a mess of purple blotches and bruises. Several of her front teeth were missing.

After her last visit with Luis, Maria had told her comrades about her new faith during a meeting of all the Communist leaders in the country. A few days later, a jeep full of her former comrades ran down Maria on the streets. The next day, several militant university students attacked her and smashed her face against a utility pole until she was unconscious. Maria was forced to hide out in the basements of several churches and in the homes of missionaries.

Luis listened to her story in amazement because she was such a young believer yet showed such courage. "There is going to be a revolution in June," she told Luis.

On the morning of the revolution, the Communist Party leader came out of hiding to talk with Maria. In a few hours, he was to become the new ruler of the country, but first he wanted to talk with his longtime friend.

"Maria," he asked, "why did you become a Christian?"

"Because I believe in God and in Jesus Christ, and my

faith has changed my life."

"You know," he said, "while hiding out, I have been listening to HCJB radio on shortwave, and they almost have me believing there is a God!"

"There is!" she said. "Why don't you become a Christian and get out of this business! We never had any real convictions about atheism and materialism. And look at all the lives we've ruined and all the terrible things we've been into. Here, take this Bible and this book (*Peace with God* by Billy Graham). You can go to my father's farm and read them."

Miraculously, he accepted her offer. Later that morning, the disturbance fizzled into chaos, and Ecuador was saved from anarchy or tyranny.

Throughout the years, Luis had seen many people come to Christ, but Maria's was one of the most dramatic stories. Yet, when Luis saw the effect of her conversion on the history of an entire country, it solidified his burden for the lost without Christ Jesus—not just for the good of individuals, but also for nations.

Chapter 7

In Colombia, Luis was growing desperate to move into city-wide evangelistic crusades. Although he didn't want to move away from OC International, he felt that maybe it would be necessary. Pastor Ray Stedman was in Guatemala for a pastors' conference and flew over to see Luis. "Be patient," was Pastor Stedman's advice.

"How long must I sit around and sit around?" Luis asked him. "If I have to leave OC and start on my own from scratch, I may do it."

"Be patient," Ray repeated. "If God is in it, it will happen when the time is right."

In late 1966, Luis prepared to attend the World Congress on Evangelism in Berlin. Just before leaving, he received some correspondence from Vic Whetzel, an OC board member. This man urged Luis to consider Mexico a fertile ground for mass evangelism. As Luis thought about the letter on the plane to Berlin, he wasn't sure what it meant.

One dark, cold afternoon when the congress meetings had let out early, many of the twelve hundred delegates were milling around West Berlin. Luis received a call from OC board members Dr. Ray Benson and Dr. Dick Hillis. The men wanted to take a walk with Luis and talk. They walked for a long time before they reached the point of their visit.

"Luis," Dick said, "we feel you and Pat should go home on furlough in December as planned. Once your furlough is over, begin to develop your own evangelistic team with your sights set on Mexico. You'll be the field director for Mexico with your headquarters there."

For once, Luis stood speechless. A dream had come true. He was grateful for the patient work from his colleagues at OC International. Then Luis asked the two men for OC team member Joe Lathrop. Dick and Ray agreed readily and asked what else could be done. Luis said he would need someone for music, so they arranged for Bruce Woodman to work with him.

Before Luis left on furlough, the OC team held their first citywide crusade in Bogota, Colombia. At the opening parade of the four-day crusade, thousands jammed the Bolivar Plaza. Even the president of Columbia came out of his office on the plaza and asked what was happening. By the time Luis spoke, twenty thousand people had jammed the plaza. Standing on the stairway of the main government building, Luis preached on "Christ the Liberator" (John 8:36).

At the end of the brief message, three hundred people raised their hands, publicly committing their lives to Jesus Christ, and several hundred more were saved during the crusade meetings over the next four nights. With these four days, Luis Palau initiated a new era for mass evangelism throughout Latin America. He was eager to see what doors would open in Mexico for the gospel of Jesus Christ.

During their work in Mexico, the Palau team heard about another religious group that had drawn a large crowd to a convention. For their next Mexico City crusade, the Palau team called it a convention. The response was overwhelming. In ten days, the crusade drew more than 106,000 people. Nearly 6,675 people committed their lives to Christ. Local churches in Mexico City doubled overnight.

In many ways, the 1970 Mexico crusade was the spark that made many people focus their attention on mass evangelism south of the U.S. border. One journalist reporting on the crusade's impact called Luis "the Billy Graham of Latin America." Others picked up the story, and the word spread. Slowly, the Palau team's dream of crusade evangelism was becoming a reality. Years of hard work and perseverance were beginning to pay off. They could reach the masses with the good news about Jesus Christ.

Early in 1971, Luis returned for a two-week crusade in Lima, Peru. The large bullring held more than 103,000 people. And nearly 5,000 people made public decisions for Jesus Christ.

Suddenly, the news media in Latin America grew interested in the Palau team. Forty-two newsmen gathered for a press conference about the crusade. It was unheard of for such a group to cover an evangelistic meeting.

Christians in Peru had been ridiculed or ignored by the media. Now the Palau team received nationwide coverage.

Parts of Luis's messages were broadcast on fifty-five radio stations. As Billy Graham had done in the United States, the Palau team began to do overseas—use interviews with the media to spread the good news about Jesus Christ.

Two years later, a twelve-day crusade was scheduled in Santo Domingo in the Dominican Republic. The Palau team invited key people in the city, including the president, to a breakfast before the crusade. The president didn't attend but sent a lawyer as his representative. After the breakfast, Luis spoke to the president's lawyer.

"The president would like to meet with you before you leave the country," she said. "But he can see you only on Sunday, immediately after mass, in the chapel of the presidential palace. If you come to mass with him, he will have forty-five minutes to talk with you. His chauffeur will pick you up at 8:30 Sunday morning."

"I'll be there!" Luis said. To Luis's knowledge, no one had ever witnessed to this man before. What an exciting opportunity for the gospel in the Dominican Republic!

After the initial excitement wore off, Luis began to worry. *Some non-Catholic Christians might hear about me sitting through mass and become upset with me. I can't go through with this.* When Luis talked with some of the pastors in Santo Domingo, they confirmed his fear about the meeting. They told him not to go.

Later, Luis consulted with a Christian lawyer who worked closely with the government. This man advised him, "You should go to mass and witness to the president." Palau knew what the Lord wanted him to do, but he turned coward. When the chauffeur arrived on Sunday morning, Luis sent him away.

Discouragement swept over him like a flood. His joy in the Lord disappeared. That afternoon Luis prayed, "Lord, forgive me. I'll never turn down an opportunity to witness to somebody because I fear what others might think."

A few years later, while visiting another South American country, Luis spoke privately with the president, a military man. "Mr. President," Luis asked, "do you know Jesus Christ?"

The president smiled and said, "Palau, I've led such a hard life; I don't think God wants to know me very much."

"Mr. President, no matter what you've done, Christ died on the cross to receive the punishment that should be ours for the wrong we have done." Luis said, "Sir, would you like to receive Christ now?"

The president paused and quite seriously said, "If Christ will receive me, I want to become a real Christian."

Right then, the men bowed their heads and prayed together. This general opened his heart to the Son of God and received Christ into his life.

The president had believed that God would never receive him because of his past. But when he and Luis finished praying, he stood up and, in the custom of his country, gave Luis a tremendous hug. "Thank you," he said. "Now I know that Christ has really received me and forgiven me."

In the months that followed, Luis spoke at other large crusades in Nicaragua, Guatemala, Chile, and Peru. Thousands of people heard the gospel and accepted Jesus Christ. Then in 1975, Luis took a break from his Latin America work and preached the good news in thirteen cities in four nations of the United Kingdom during a two-week period. Luis became convinced that God was calling him to evangelize the British Isles as well as Latin America.

About this time, *Time* magazine reported that Latin America was turning to Christ with one exception: the country of Uruguay. Fully thirty percent of its people claimed to be atheists—a figure that was unheard of outside the communist world. Luis determined to proclaim the gospel in this country.

Flying from city to city in Uruguay was impossible, so Luis and his team traveled in an assortment of older vehicles over sixteen hundred miles of roads to present the gospel to more than one hundred thousand men, women, and young people. The six back-to-back crusades were exhausting, but the team was encouraged at the response to the gospel.

After preaching throughout Uruguay, Luis returned to OC International board meetings in California. He had accepted the presidency with the condition that it would be reviewed in two years. After prayerful consideration, Luis asked the board to release him from his OC leadership responsibilities. He found it impossible to manage his thirty-member evangelistic team and also lead the mission.

Everyone on the board agreed that it would be best if

the Luis Palau Evangelistic Association (LPEA) became a separate missions organization. Effective October 1, 1978, the organization was started, and Luis Palau began a new ministry with headquarters in Portland, Oregon, where he and Pat had first met and married.

A couple of weeks after LPEA became a separate organization, Luis and the team returned to Bolivia for three weeks of meetings. Although some amazing results had happened four years earlier, nothing could have prepared them for the national revival in October 1978.

In La Paz, the capital city, police had to close the stadium gates each night. They turned hundreds of people away from the public crusade meetings. On Saturday and Sunday, two services were held each afternoon and evening. The lines of people stretched for blocks to enter the stadium.

In Santa Cruz and Cochabamba, Bolivia, an overwhelming response also happened. During the crusade, they broke nearly every previous Luis Palau crusade record—for attendance (180,000), decisions for Christ (18,916), and the ratio of decisions to attendance (10.5 percent).

Throughout Bolivia, many stories were told about changed lives as people received Christ. But two decisions were unforgettable for Luis and probably weren't in the crusade statistics.

At a midmorning press conference in a prestigious downtown La Paz hotel, journalists' pens were scratching the news. Luis began answering questions—sometimes barbed—from some of Bolivia's leading editors and writers. A little girl slipped into the room. Luis recognized her as the daughter of the hotel elevator operator and thought, *What could she possibly want?*

He picked up a copy of one of his books and autographed it, then handed it to the girl and whispered, "The Lord bless you, Sweetheart." He smiled at the girl, but she held her ground. She didn't want a book and a smile.

"Mr. Palau, what I really wanted to ask you was how I could receive Jesus in my heart." The previous evening, the girl, who looked less than eleven years old, had watched Palau counsel people on national television. He spoke to a high school student and led him to Christ. Now she, too, wanted to receive the Savior.

Instantly the plans for the press conference evaporated. Quickly, Luis asked the media to leave the room. Publicity was important to the crusade, but Palau knew the reporters could ask their questions another day. As 2 Corinthians 6:2 says, "Now is the day of salvation."

While in Bolivia, the team held another President's Prayer Breakfast with Bolivia's new president, General Juan Pereda Asbun, twenty-five high-ranking military officers, eight cabinet members, and many other leaders.

During a twenty-minute address, Palau read Deuteronomy 28:1–14, then outlined the national benefits when a country obeys the Lord. In response, President Pereda stood up and reaffirmed the importance of setting "personal and national spiritual priorities." Then the president publicly endorsed the crusades.

Afterward, in a private meeting, Luis asked the president about his own relationship with Jesus Christ, then explained the good news of forgiveness through the blood of Jesus Christ. There in his presidential office, President Pereda bowed his head and gave his life to Christ. The social position of a person didn't matter to Luis. For him, there was no greater thrill than to lead someone to Christ.

A few weeks later, thousands more trusted Christ in Acapulco and Veracruz, Mexico. Luis felt God's call on his life and the Lord's blessing on his team.

As the 1970s drew to a close, Palau and his team held meetings in Caracas, Venezuela, as well as fifteen youth rallies in ten cities of England during two weeks. More than 2,700 people registered their commitment to Jesus Christ. Many leading evangelicals in Britain talked with Luis about the dismal trend of the church in Great Britain. Churches were closing by the hundreds, and often church furnishings were shipped to America, Japan, and Western Europe to be sold as antiques.

Luis thought, *If it takes a third-generation transplanted European who was born in the Third World and who now claims American citizenship to help turn the tide in Britain, so be it.*

The next spring, Palau and his team returned to England for another series of crusades in Scotland. In a week and a half, nearly two thousand people committed their lives to Christ.

Behind closed doors, a dozen Scottish ministers met with Luis. They voiced their opposition to his organized mass evangelism. As they talked, Luis was surprised by the differences they had over basic questions. At least half of the ministers honestly told Luis that they didn't accept the Bible as the trustworthy Word of God. Was it any surprise that churches throughout this region were failing? Thousands of people's lives were transformed through the gospel message from the Palau team.

Later that year, Luis traveled to Guayaquil, Ecuador, for a crusade. After the evening meetings, the live call-in counseling program was broadcast for twelve consecutive nights over twenty-five repeater stations to all of Ecuador and much of neighboring Colombia and Peru. More than 2,800 made decisions for Christ at the Guayaquil crusade, and only heaven will know the results from the call-in counseling. When the nightly broadcasts stopped, 180 people called in to complain. They didn't want the program to end. This type of response was unheard of for almost any other kind of programming!

Back in the U.S., Pat Palau was fighting the battle of her life against breast cancer, so Luis cut back on his travel schedule. Luis began to think, *With Pat so sick, why not make more extensive use of the media this next year?* That would give him more time to be available to his wife. His team members agreed.

Besides Pat's ongoing cancer treatments, there were other

reasons for Luis to curtail his crusade schedule. Pat told Luis, "If you don't stay at home, these boys will go straight to the world." He panicked to think of his sons walking away from the Lord. He spent some time at home in Portland, Oregon.

Together Pat and Luis decided to watch Kevin and Keith for the next six months. If they saw no change, Luis would drop all of his crusade commitments. It was a desperate decision, but they didn't see any other option.

Soon after that, Christian musician Keith Green came to Portland. Keith and Kevin attended his concert and a retreat. They were both deeply moved and dedicated their lives to God. Shortly after this experience, they applied to Wheaton College, a leading Christian school. Luis and Pat breathed a sigh of relief. But the struggles continued.

Because of Pat's ongoing battle with cancer, Luis cut back his 1981 crusade schedule to two crusades. He traveled to Glasgow, Scotland, for five weeks as a part of the LPEA three-year strategy to reevangelize Scotland. During the thirty-six day crusade, more than 5,325 people committed their lives to Jesus Christ. Evangelism was back on the map in Scotland.

After the Scotland crusade, Luis thought about evangelism in America. Ever since he had first felt God's call to crusade evangelism, Palau had poured himself into overseas evangelism. He planned to stay out of the States until Billy Graham slowed down. That was twenty years ago and Billy Graham was still going as strong as ever. Luis wondered when he would get a chance. *Is my dream of evangelizing America's cities always going to be only a dream?* he wondered.

With some hesitation, he accepted an invitation to San Diego for LPEA's first full-scale American crusade. More than twelve hundred people committed their lives to Christ during the crusade, but Luis felt that somehow he had disobeyed the Lord. Yes, the Lord was opening the door of opportunity for ministry in the United States, but it would be on God's schedule—not Luis's.

That fall, Kevin and Keith flew out of the nest for their first semester at Wheaton College, near Chicago. A few days after they returned home for the holidays, a bone scan revealed Pat had no signs of cancer. The Palau family celebrated Christmas and New Year's in a big way that year.

The next year, Luis started with a new level of intensity. Seven crusades were scheduled on four continents. He made trips to the countries of Australia, Finland, Paraguay, England, and Guatemala, and to the states of Washington and Wisconsin.

The series of crusades in Guatemala City was held in conjunction with the hundred-year celebration of the good news coming to the nation. A few months earlier, the LPEA team had wondered if the celebration would be canceled because of political violence. But after months of upheaval, finally Guatemala was enjoying a period of relative peace. The Central American field director, Benjamin Orozco, assured Luis that the crusade could proceed as planned without incident.

The weeklong crusade received more media attention than any of the previous 175 crusades and rallies. Each night, fifteen radio stations broadcast the messages live from the crusade. More than twenty evangelistic messages that Luis had taped aired on two television stations.

Early one Sunday, hundreds of Christians prepared to celebrate one hundred years of the gospel in their country. Before this celebration, no one knew how many committed Christians were in Guatemala. For years, Luis had been saying that it would be the first nation to achieve fifty-one percent of born-again Christians. But nothing could have prepared Luis for what he and his team saw that morning.

Tens of thousands, then hundreds of thousands of people started to fill the park. Military helicopters flew overhead, trying to get some estimate of the crowd size—first 500,000, then 600,000, finally 700,000 people! After the event, historian Virgil Zapara called it the largest gathering of born-again Christians in the history not only of Guatemala, but of all Latin America. The largest gathering of the church in Guatemala reaffirmed Luis's belief in mass evangelism and its effectiveness.

His call to evangelistic work was clear from the Scriptures, church history, and experience, but it was not without critics. Some people have severely criticized Luis Palau and others for meeting with presidents, prime ministers, and other top government officials. Luis clearly believes that everyone needs the healing power and freedom of a personal relationship with Jesus Christ—including the leaders of nations.

Over the next several years, Luis and his team continued to focus on ministry overseas. They had three crusades in America during three years and planned to have five more over the next five years. But the green light was flashing in other countries.

In the fall of 1983, the Palau Association blanketed London with nine regional crusades and an ambitious seven-week crusade six months later. At the Mission to London, Luis preached every night for six weeks in Queen's Park Ranger's Stadium. People from every creed, color, religious background, and walk of life trusted Jesus Christ—a top rock star, a famous actress, a disillusioned policeman, a car dealer, a truck driver, and a bus driver were interviewed on the same night by the BBC.

The official crusade photographer, an Australian soccer player, a young businesswoman, a gentleman whose wife had prayed for his salvation for twenty-one years, twenty-five boys at a British boarding school, a young gang member who had helped disrupt the meeting earlier that same evening, a runaway teenager, and more than a few religious ministers also made decisions for Jesus Christ.

By the final night, the cumulative attendance for the Mission to London had topped 518,000, and more than 28,000 people had made public commitments to Jesus Christ. The last week of June, Luis's messages were broadcast to the entire British Commonwealth—fifty nations.

Beyond this huge effort to bring the gospel to the British Commonwealth, the Palau team also had similar missions to Latin America in 1985 and Asia in 1986. They saw tremendous results.

Sometimes the Palau team is accused of talking too much about numbers. In many parts of the world, people are being born by the thousands and dying by the thousands. But as Luis says, they are being won to Jesus Christ by ones and twos. As the Palau team reaches the masses, they want to give exclusive glory to God for His moving in the hearts of men and women through the presentation of the good news about Jesus Christ.

During 1985, Vice President George Bush and Luis spoke to students at Wheaton College. Both men received honorary doctorates during the commencement exercises. For Luis, the degree marked his second honorary doctorate. He received the first one from Talbot Theological Seminary in 1977. At the Wheaton ceremony, Luis found it a special moment because that day his twin sons, Keith and Kevin, graduated with honors.

Over the next months, Luis and his team saw amazing results for the gospel during crusades in Switzerland and Argentina. Returning home, he poured himself into his final preparations for the first Asian crusade in Singapore.

As Luis preached in the National Stadium of Singapore,

his messages were broadcast through a cooperative effort with Far East Broadcasting Company, Trans World Radio, HCJB, and other missionary radio and television ministries. The meetings were simultaneously translated into eight major Asian languages and broadcast throughout Asia.

During the meetings, 11,902 people publicly gave their lives to Jesus Christ. After the meetings, Luis and the team received invitations for other crusades in Hong Kong, India, Indonesia, Japan, the Philippines, Thailand, and other Asian nations. An opportunity for ministry was opening to Luis and the team in a different part of the world.

Early the next year, Luis went to Fiji and New Zealand in the South Pacific to conduct four weeks of crusades. These were hard days of intense meetings for Luis. Four to six daily events drained his energy, and his voice was practically gone. There wasn't a single day's break in four weeks. During these days of ministry, 11,426 people committed their lives to Jesus Christ. With results like that, Luis found his energy renewed for mass evangelism.

Also that spring, Luis preached the good news for the first time in Africa. He went to Nairobi, Kenya, and preached at a one-night evangelistic rally. Three hundred and fifty people accepted the Lord.

During this time, Luis received the first of many invitations to preach the gospel in Eastern Europe. As the Iron Curtain fell, Luis and his team found many people hungry for the good news of salvation through Christ. Little did he know that, during the next four years, he would personally see more than 101,000 Eastern Europeans commit their lives to Jesus Christ. The doors of ministry were opening wider and wider for Luis Palau.

As Luis and his team geared up to finish the 1980s with a flurry of crusades, Luis continued to turn his heart and thoughts toward home. He had studied the rise and fall of Christianity in western civilization. He saw that America was in between the midcentury revival of Christianity and total secularism.

While preaching in other nations, Luis felt that he could no longer ignore crusade invitations in the United States. His team must go to the nations of the world but also to America—not immediately, but in an organized, planned strategy under the guidance of the Spirit of the Lord.

Luis's burden for America increased as he and the team had another crusade in Guatemala. Nearly 250,000 people packed Mateo Flores Stadium to hear the gospel. Even more people crowded on a nearby hillside. More than 6,600 people made a public commitment to Jesus Christ, and another 1,600 did the same at precrusade events.

Despite his growing concern for America, Luis didn't want to move ahead without talking to Billy Graham. For some reason, he felt nervous about calling the older evangelist.

Much to Luis's surprise, a couple weeks later, Billy Graham called him in Los Angeles. Luis still doesn't know how Billy Graham got the phone number.

"Luis," he said, "I just saw that article in *Christianity Today*." The article spoke about the recent Palau team crusades. They had just returned from Poland and Hungary, and they had accepted invitations to preach the gospel in the first public stadium evangelistic crusades in the history of the Soviet Union.

"Goodness gracious," Billy exclaimed. "You're all over the world these days."

Luis took a deep breath and then began. "Billy, I've got to ask your blessing on something." Then Luis explained his long-standing burden for America. "I feel the time has come that I should accept more crusade invitations in the States and really go for the bigger cities. But I want to feel that I have your full blessing."

Billy said, "Well, you don't need it. But if you want it, you've got it. Get on with it! Everybody talks about evangelizing America. Now let's really do it."

Luis knew Billy was right. If Palau had to describe the situation in America with one word, it would be confusion. According to Gallup Polls, nine out of ten Americans believed in God. Eight out of ten called themselves Christians. Four out of ten claimed they went to church on any given Sunday. But Luis wondered, *Where is the reality? Where is the witness to a watching world?*

That April, the LPEA board of directors mandated that the Palau Evangelistic Association begin accepting invitations for as many as four American metropolitan area crusades a year. Ironically, Palau and his team received this mandate with the knowledge of commitments for crusades in many other places in the world.

In the middle of August, Luis and several team members said an earnest prayer for safety before flying to Bogota, Colombia. In a forty-eight-hour period, a number of political assassinations had taken place, including the killing of the leading presidential candidate.

The drug cartel had declared an all-out war. In the middle of one of Colombia's worst crises, Palau preached the good news about Jesus Christ to capacity crowds. The team saw an incredible 10,288 people dedicate their lives to the Lord that week.

A few weeks later, Luis and his team arrived in the Soviet Union for a historic series of meetings in four republics. They received a telegram from Billy Graham that said, "We are praying that God will abundantly bless you and that many people will find Christ. We are praying that your meetings will open doors for others that may come later." Luis felt thankful for the wonderful friend that Billy Graham had become to him.

That Christmas marked the first time that the Palau family wasn't together since the twins had been born. The third Palau son, Andrew, had graduated from the University of Oregon and moved to Boston to "seek his fortune." Pat and Luis had unvoiced concerns about whether Andrew intended to walk with the Lord, but there was little they could do.

They committed Andrew to the Lord, kept the lines of communication open, loved him, and continued praying.

During the first part of 1992, Luis and the team continued a fast-paced tour throughout the United Kingdom. As his theme, Luis talked about the need of today's church—the mighty fire of the Holy Spirit. Palau said, "As Christians, the Holy Spirit's fire is in us. We must not let that fire die down!" Instead, he encouraged the believers to "fan into flame the gift of God, which is in you" (2 Timothy 1:6, NIV).

Throughout the years, Luis has spoken to many different gatherings such as Urbana and National Prayer Breakfasts, and conventions of the National Religious Broadcasters and the Evangelical Press Association. But in the summer of 1992, Luis was one of the speakers at the first Promise Keepers conference in Boulder, Colorado. As he saw tens of thousands of Christian men commit themselves to be godly men of integrity, it gave him hope for America's spiritual revival. He thought, *God is about to do something great through this movement in our land!*

On the border of the United States, the Palau team held a crusade in Reynosa, Mexico. Mayor Ramon Perez Garcia welcomed the team to his city of 750,000 people. On the opening night of the crusade, Mayor Perez named Luis a guest of honor before a near capacity crowd of 14,000 people. "What energy we have here!" he said to Luis.

"It's the energy of God," Palau responded.

"Yes, yes," the mayor replied. That evening, his wife

came forward to receive Christ.

On the other side of the Rio Grande in McAllen, Texas, area churches united for a series of meetings with Luis Palau. The four rallies in Memorial Stadium were attended by 32,500 people. The live call-in counseling program called *Night Talk* preempted *The Tonight Show* with Jay Leno on the NBC affiliate. Nine people prayed with Luis on the air to receive Jesus Christ as their Savior. In the studio, two cameramen and a control room operator also trusted in Christ.

In ten days in the Rio Grande Valley, more than 5,400 people made a public declaration of their lives to Christ. That fall, thousands more were brought into God's kingdom during crusades in Panama, Portugal, and Phoenix.

At the Phoenix crusade press conference in the America West Arena, Jerry Colangelo, the owner of the NBA Phoenix Suns, introduced Luis Palau. Luis spoke of his desire to bring America back to her days of glory. "A spirit of despondency seems to permeate this nation," he explained. "Our currency says, 'In God We Trust,' but we have gotten away from trusting God. Americans have lost hope."

Then Luis continued on the theme of reconciliation. "We need to get over this business of being hyphenated Americans," he said. "I've been an American for thirty years. My passport doesn't say Hispanic-American. It says citizen of the United States of America." Then he called on Americans to restore a spirit of holiness and restore their sense of what is right and good.

Finally Luis said, "America needs good news, not good advice. My dream is that people from other nations will look at a revived America and ask, 'What is happening there?' And the answer they will hear: 'A nation has been turned around, and God did it.'"

As the doors to America continued opening to the Palau team, Luis continued to be concerned about his third son, Andrew. Pat later said of their son, "I had a sense from the Lord that he was a sweet guy but had not come to Christ."

When Luis prepared in 1993 to speak at the Jamaica crusade, the Palaus invited Andrew to take a vacation from his job in Boston. They knew Andrew loved to fish, and he agreed to come to Jamaica.

During fifteen days in eleven cities, more than 245,000 people attended the meetings. Andrew came to every single meeting. One night, Andrew walked forward with the people to recommit his life to Jesus Christ.

Besides deep-sea fishing, Andrew discovered something else in Jamaica—a lovely girl named Wendy. A few months after the crusade, Wendy invited Andrew to a Christian retreat. During this retreat, Andrew poured out his past to the Lord and received forgiveness. In 1994, Andrew and Wendy were married. Andrew has been working part-time with LPEA and attending graduate school at Multnomah. He worked with LPEA on the preparations for the eight-week Say Yes Crusade in Chicago in April and May of 1996.

Luis said, "To me, Andrew's conversion is a beautiful picture of what I'd like to see God do for the people of America, young and old. There are thousands of other Andrews who need Jesus Christ. My heart goes out to them—and to their families."

Through more than thirty years of mass evangelism, Luis Palau has personally addressed more than twelve million people. More than 700,000 people have made known decisions for Jesus Christ during some 360 crusades and rallies. He has an estimated daily radio audience of twenty-two million people. In addition, he's testing a national weekly evangelistic television outreach that could reach millions more with the gospel.

Luis says, "With all my heart, I'm convinced the resurrected Lord Jesus Christ has the power to effect massive positive changes in America." The years ahead will show what further part Luis Palau will have in bringing that message to America and the rest of the world.

If you enjoyed

MODERN HEROES,

check out these other great
Backpack Books!

GIRLS' CLASSICS
Including *Pocahontas,*
Little Women,
Heidi, and *Pollyanna*

BIBLE HEROES
Including *Noah, Joseph,*
David, and *Daniel*

BIBLE HEROINES
Including *Deborah, Ruth,*
Esther, and *Mary*

GOD'S AMBASSADORS
Including *Hudson Taylor,*
David Livingstone,
Gladys Aylward,
and *Jim Elliot*

CHRISTIAN ADVENTURES
Including *Ben-Hur,*
The Pilgrim's Progress,
Robinson Crusoe, and
The Swiss Family Robinson

AMERICAN HEROES
Including
Roger Williams,
Abraham Lincoln,
Harriet Tubman,
and *Clara Barton*

THE SON OF GOD
Including *Jesus,*
The Miracles of Jesus,
The Parables of Jesus,
and *The Twelve Disciples*

Great reading at a great price—only $3.97 each!

Available wherever books are sold.
Or order from
Barbour Publishing, Inc.
P.O. Box 719
Uhrichsville, Ohio 44683

If ordering by mail,
please add $2.00 to your order for shipping and handling.
Prices are subject to change without notice.